THE
LITTLE
ORANGE
BOOK II

THE LITTLE ORANGE BOOK II

STUDENT VOICES ON
EXCELLENT TEACHING

THE UNIVERSITY OF TEXAS SYSTEM
Academy of Distinguished Teachers

cooperation innovation assessment engagement collaboration
creativity mentorship technique development sharing skills
daring foresight growth learning technology communication

DISTRIBUTED BY TOWER BOOKS
AN IMPRINT OF THE UNIVERSITY OF TEXAS PRESS

Requests for permission to reproduce material from this work should
be sent to:
    Permissions
    University of Texas Press
    P.O. Box 7819
    Austin, TX 78713-7819
    utpress.utexas.edu/rp-form

♾ The paper used in this book meets the minimum requirements of
ANSI/NISO Z39.48-1992 (R1997) (Permanence of Paper).

LIBRARY OF CONGRESS CATALOGING-IN-PUBLICATION DATA
Names: University of Texas System. Academy of Distinguished
    Teachers. Title: The little orange book II : student voices on
    excellent teaching / the University of Texas System, Academy of
    Distinguished Teachers. Other titles: Little orange book two
Description: First edition. | Austin : Tower Books, an imprint of the
    University of Texas Press, 2020.
Identifiers: LCCN 2019022665
    ISBN 978-1-4773-1538-5 (cloth)
Subjects: LCSH: Teaching. | Effective teaching. | College students—
    Attitudes.
Classification: LCC LB1025.3 .L573 2020 | DDC 371.102—dc23
LC record available at https://lccn.loc.gov/2019022665

doi:10.7560/315385

CONTENTS

INTRODUCTION

TEACHING IS A POWERFUL PROFESSION, and learning is a noble pursuit. No matter the setting in which teaching and learning occur—in a classroom, in a lab, online, or elsewhere—the combination of dedicated teachers and engaged students has the potential to transform lives.

The Little Orange Book: Short Lessons in Excellent Teaching provided effective teaching strategies written by university faculty members. *The Little Orange Book II: Student Voices on Excellent Teaching* features the voices of our students. The premise for this book came from two seemingly simple questions: What makes a good student? What makes a good teacher? The students who responded to our questions provided a wide range of thoughtful responses. No one suggested that getting an A in a class was the singular mark of a good student. Rather, characteristics such as dedication, openness, curiosity, risk taking, and hard work were often mentioned. Similarly, students described good teachers as those who demonstrate passion toward the subject matter and a caring attitude toward their students' success and well-being.

The book was developed by the thirty-three members of the University of Texas System Academy of Distinguished

Teachers. This group represents the most accomplished and renowned teachers from across the UT System with its eight academic campuses and over 200,000 students. Each campus has some shade of orange as its chosen school color, inspiring the title of this volume, but of course the pieces are relevant far beyond the Lone Star State.

Most of the chapters of *The Little Orange Book II: Student Voices on Excellent Teaching* were written by students enrolled in one of the eight UT System academic campuses. The student essays are organized into chapters and are introduced by a member of the Academy of Distinguished Teachers. Intermixed are short statements and questions intended to provoke thought, reflection, discussion, and inspiration. Following these are essays written by each campus president. We asked our presidents to share their thoughts, stories, and experiences about powerful teaching moments from the student perspective. What results is a rich tapestry of student, faculty, and university president voices about the impact that caring, passionate, and thoughtful teaching can have on both validating and transforming the lives of students.

We hope the readers of this volume will also take a moment to reflect on what they believe to be the qualities of good teaching and learning and consider how each time they find themselves in a teaching or learning environment, they, too, will be inspired.

BETH BRUNK-CHAVEZ
PRESIDENT, UT SYSTEM ACADEMY
OF DISTINGUISHED TEACHERS

GREAT TEACHERS

GREAT PROFESSORS HELP
MAKE GREAT STUDENTS

THERE ARE SEVERAL CHARACTERISTICS that most professors would agree make a great student. Great students are typically intrinsically motivated; they are driven to truly learn and understand. While grades are important to them, great students are not driven solely or predominantly by grades. This is a very important characteristic because professors want to believe that students are as interested and motivated about the course material as they are.

Another related characteristic of a great student is exhibiting passion and enthusiasm for learning. Great students are excited about going to class and never want to miss a class if they can help it. They look forward to what the teacher is presenting in each class. They come prepared, having done their readings and other class assignments. They are active participants in class. Note that there is no mention of how well they are doing in the class. While it is often assumed that great students are straight-A students, or close to that, a broader understanding of great students is needed when teaching students of diverse learning needs.

We could easily continue focusing on the individual

characteristics of great students, including being open-minded and respectful, hardworking, and goal-oriented; wanting to be a great student; and being conscientious. All professors would agree about these characteristics and would likely prefer to see them in the students they teach.

And, of course, the question of what makes a great student often places the onus of responsibility squarely on the students, ignoring the quality of the student-faculty relationship. But in reality, great professors help make great students. What do I mean by this?

My pedagogical philosophy is that fundamentally all students want to learn. This belief may seem to contradict the experiences of some professors, who sometimes ascribe negative psychological characteristics to students (e.g., "They don't care about school," or "They don't want to learn"). This can be true even of "great" professors.

As challenging as it may be, professors must be able to look beyond the superficial and see the potential for every student to be a great student. It is this abounding optimism on the part of professors that can help students, even challenging students, realize their potential.

We know from the literature that how faculty members treat students is important in facilitating student development. Students may enter college as great students, or may have the potential to be great students. However, the nature of their interactions with professors can either promote or hinder their development.

Students can become great when they experience a caring attitude from professors. They can become great when they experience respectful interactions with their professors. Students can also become great when they experience a sense of connectedness to professors. They can become great when they experience their professors as approachable.

Great students take the time to interact with professors outside of the classroom. They take advantage of professors' office hours. These instances allow for the cultivation of positive student-professor interactions, which can contribute to the making of a great student.

This understanding of great students is radically different from focusing on students' individual characteristics. To be sure, the aforementioned individual characteristics are important and desirable. However, we run the risk of disproportionately focusing solely on what students bring to the classroom if we do not consider what professors bring to the classroom as well, and how professors contribute to the making of great students.

KEVIN COKLEY, PHD
UT SYSTEM ACADEMY OF DISTINGUISHED TEACHERS
THE UNIVERSITY OF TEXAS AT AUSTIN

HOW TO IMPACT A LIFE

I GREW UP having great admiration for the teaching profession. My mother has served as a dedicated bilingual
teacher since we moved to the United States fourteen years
ago, and she taught me that, while teachers have high expectations for their students, students should also have
high expectations of their teachers. This expectation helps
to create a positive teacher/learner relationship, a relationship that involves a shared trust, an open channel of communication, and clarity in terms of expectations. This
foundation allows for the teacher and student to be able to
handle the inevitable bumps along the road.

Following my mother's guidelines has made my school
and classroom experiences both positive and rewarding.
Every student, including me, has faced challenges with
coursework. I know from my own experience that students
who engage in class are more willing to step out of their
comfort zones and seek help from the teacher, and that
they will be rewarded with support and insights that might
otherwise be missed. The teacher, in turn, gets to know the
student's work ethic and personality, and learns how to per-
sonalize the help they offer. Therefore, a positive teacher/

> It's the teachers with a positive attitude, who have encouraged me and inspired engagement, that I remember as truly impactful.

learner experience requires effort from both the student and the teacher.

I think everyone has had "bad" teacher experiences at some point in their schooling: teachers who load up students with pointless extra readings, who drop exams and quizzes unannounced, and who ridicule a student in front of the class merely for a laugh. While I have several personal stories of bad experiences, at the end of the day it's the teachers with a positive attitude, who have encouraged me and inspired engagement, that I remember as truly impactful. One of the best teachers I had in high school didn't teach my favorite subject; nevertheless, she made Art History a class I looked forward to every day. What stood out was her engaging personality and love of the subject, which made even innumerable sculptures of ancient cement vases meaningful and thought-provoking. My senior AP Biology class was taught by a gifted PhD in immunology, who took us on a daily journey of her experiences in the lab and gave us a sense of the *eureka* moment of discovery. Near the end of my senior year, when I was struggling with which college to attend, she encouraged me to follow my dreams and aspirations, just as she did as a student.

So here I am: a first-year student at the university of my dreams, inspired by yet another amazing professor. This faculty member took all of us in his class on an inspiring journey of how infectious diseases have impacted the world (e.g., societies, religion, governments, and health), and I now find myself fascinated with the subject and eager to learn more. Beyond the classroom, his engagement with the class—for example, through dinner and an inspiring excursion to the top of the UT Tower—has demonstrated his passion for the students. The recommendation letter he wrote for me showed that he really did take the time to get to know me, and letters of support like this, from him and others, have provided me with opportunities that are enriching my experience and expanding my horizons.

While I am grateful to faculty who have provided those letters, along with emotional and academic support and the occasional moment of tough love, it is those personal connections that I will cherish the most: sharing a view of the Austin skyline from the top of the tower, or receiving congratulatory comments on Facebook for some accomplishment. I encourage all teachers to take the time to make their classroom a more personable space for each and every one of their students. The teacher not only makes or breaks the class, but the impact can last for a lifetime.

MARIAGRAZIA ARATA
THE UNIVERSITY OF TEXAS AT AUSTIN

What do you teach students that
isn't part of the curriculum?

PURE LEARNING

THE QUESTION AT HAND is what makes a great teacher. There are countless possible answers. In my experience thus far in college, as well as in life, there is no explicit set of traits that add up to a great teacher. Professors employ diverse stylistic approaches, and I have come to relish my exposure to varying teaching methods and personalities. I know that each one is transforming me in some way. But all of my great teachers have possessed a few principal qualities as the basis of their approach as educators.

The chief attribute that a great teacher demonstrates is real-world experience. The educators that I have learned the most from have all been able to provide experiences from the workplace and explain how the subject at hand applies in real life. The next characteristic is competence. Competence carries a great deal of weight in the classroom. I know that every student has had at least one instructor who has captivated and commanded the room simply by presenting information with a confidence that can only come from actual experience and the knowledge that goes along with it.

Additionally, an educator exhibits enthusiasm about

teaching and about his or her students. Teachers with this quality are able to provoke laudable responses from students in profound ways. I am elated whenever I come across teachers like this, largely because it makes me eager to come to class and enables me to learn with a more attentive mindset. Moreover, it allows the class to be conducted in a way that promotes an interactive atmosphere. Professors who educate with zeal organically incite the students to ask more questions, which leads them to take further interest in the class, and perhaps even in the field of study.

Lastly, a great teacher is able to recognize the audience and communicate to them clearly. Instructors who are able to perceive the pulse of their students are capable of teaching them anything. Students learn in different ways, and when a teacher is able to display flexible communication strategies, it is invaluable to the overall success of a learner.

> Instructors who are able to perceive the pulse of their students are capable of teaching them anything.

I feel that my chances of success greatly increase when I am able to comfortably and effectively communicate with my instructor. The majority of my memorable discussions with my past professors have also involved receiving constructive feedback on how I could improve in my future studies. This may be the most difficult trait to find in a professor, as it takes a great deal of interactive skills coupled with self-awareness.

The responses to the question of what makes a great teacher may be vast and varied. But the handful of great teachers I've had the privilege of knowing have all demonstrated the aforementioned qualities. Every student is different and will have a different idea about the skill set desired in a teacher. However, it is only when an educator places the quality of the students' academic learning before themselves that pure learning can take place.

CARL RYAN ROBINS
THE UNIVERSITY OF TEXAS AT EL PASO

Do your students know how many
minutes are left until class is over?

REAL-TIME TEACHING
IN THREE DIMENSIONS

A GOOD TEACHING ENVIRONMENT is malleable. An overreliance on any one feature can diminish the learning experience as a whole. For example, the slate was originally a wonderful tool for students, allowing even impoverished communities to practice writing without pen, pencil, or even paper. As funding for education increased, the slates got bigger and became the intimidating blackboard, hung at the front of every twentieth-century classroom, drawing the fixed attention of the students and forcing the educator into a sort of two-dimensional performance. The lecture, as it came to be known, was much inferior to one-on-one instruction, but it continues to dominate class time in the new millennium.

Even as the medium of presentation changed—from chalkboard to projector screen—the organization of the seats in a classroom remained the same: rigid rows all facing toward one wall. Many auditorium-sized classrooms at universities have the same complex and cramped plastic seating as the cheapest of high school auditoriums, with a desk surface awkwardly forced in. Certain professors, in a touch of ironic fundamentalism, teach in a style harkening back to the earliest forms of abstract education in Western history, holding Socratic seminars in which the students are arranged in an inward-facing circle. This design, however, is complicated again by the success of education in marketing itself: there are just too many students to be educated for such a circle to be meaningfully representative of each student's own voice. Some will obviously dominate the discussion more than others as class sizes grow beyond fifteen; at twenty-five students in a circle, roughly a third will actively check out of their surroundings and focus on their phones or their fingernails rather than taking part in the discussion. And if there are windows on more than one side of the classroom, that number will jump to half. They need something to keep their focus—like, say, a chalkboard. And we are back where we started.

The key to a good teaching environment is to avoid becoming attached to one format for a classroom. Today's next big thing is to-

> A good teaching environment is malleable.

morrow's uncomfortable arrangement. Instead, the content of a class should be able to engage students from a host of angles and with any number of learning props or lack thereof. Many students in the Millennial generation are used to being treated as having the attention span of gerbils and requiring flashy PowerPoint transitions to maintain their focus. When a class has no prepared slides or displayed information, a part of the students' minds that they have not used in a long time becomes active. Instead of trying to copy everything the professor writes on the chalkboard or presents on the projector screen, the students will learn to listen and discern the important topics without pointed guides. Some will get lost. But many students will find themselves energized and awake in class in a way they were not before when simply copying notes. Even if the classroom is dominated by a chalkboard or projector, the professor can still appeal to the pure abstraction of language to get her point across to students without spelling it out on a big screen. For this is how knowledge is turned into wisdom, not by passing the facts whole from the mind of the teacher to the minds of the students, but by training the minds of the students to discern the facts for themselves.

JOHN MARTIN CROWLEY
THE UNIVERSITY OF TEXAS AT ARLINGTON

*How does your class contribute
to your students' lives?*

THE HIGHEST CALLING

I AM PRIVILEGED to have been taught by some of what I believe to be the most exceptional professors on our—or on any—campus. Although each one does so in a slightly different way, these professors inspire their students with the same judicious mixture of strength, flexibility, and guidance—a perfect blend of motivation and support that continues to serve students long after the graduation ceremony has ended. It is this effective, three-fold combination of teaching principles that stands out as an exemplar for all professors to follow, and it is one that I hope to emulate in my own teaching endeavors.

An effective professor will go the extra mile to ensure that students have the necessary tools to succeed in the classroom. Knowing that students need a structured form of instruction and guidance, the successful professor will provide detailed information concerning course requirements. Without such information, students will often miss deadlines and will fall short of expectations, leading to a sense of failure and inadequacy that can prove detrimental to the student's fu-

> An effective professor will go the extra mile to ensure that students have the necessary tools to succeed.

ture success. In contrast, when professors provide their students with set guidelines, the students become aware of classroom goals and expectations and can take the necessary steps to meet course requirements.

Yet classroom requirements alone are not enough to properly guide a student in the right direction. A certain amount of flexibility is necessary to gauge whether the classroom guidelines are functioning as expected. Oftentimes, what works on paper is not effective in practice. A truly great professor will neither be afraid—nor too proud—to make necessary adjustments to classroom requirements in favor of student learning. In perhaps one of the boldest moves of this type that I have observed, the professor decreased the amount of assigned classroom reading materials by half. The professor wisely noted that the students were struggling to complete lengthy readings at the expense of comprehension and analysis—skills that would be a greater long-term benefit to students. Following the schedule change, the students gained a much deeper understanding of the readings and developed skills that will serve them well in the workplace.

In addition, a truly great professor will become a guide—a mentor—to his or her students. A professor who sacrifices time outside of the classroom to personally direct and encourage a student in his or her academic endeavors can rest assured that such efforts will not be in vain. The professor's personal investment will bring tangible rewards. As the student gains experience and knowledge, he or she will likely become a mentor to others, continuing the cycle indefinitely.

The finest professors are those who value their students'

success above their own—those who have answered the call to teach and inspire the minds of others. These professors hold in their hands the keys to student success—keys that, for students, unlock the door to a world of opportunity that extends far beyond the classroom walls.

CAROL DEGRASSE
THE UNIVERSITY OF TEXAS AT TYLER

*How long does it take
to become a great teacher?*

A MEANINGFUL AND
LASTING IMPRESSION

TO MANY STUDENTS, sitting in a classroom daily may seem dull, pointless, and time-consuming. Often, students sit in their chairs counting down the minutes until class ends. Daydreaming and sleeping are typical among students when a class fails to excite them or keep their interest. However, the classroom experience has the capability of being enhanced by a single person, the teacher. Teachers have the opportunity to leave a lasting impression on their students and create an environment for all to enjoy. For this reason, the question of what makes a great teacher and the question of what makes a memorable class or learning experience go hand-in-hand.

What makes a great teacher? This question has a number of possible answers, but most students may answer in a similar manner. A college friend of mine once told me that she would never forget her fourth-grade teacher. When I asked her why, she explained that her teacher's simple questions, like "How are you today?" or "Is there anything giving you trouble that I might be able to help with?," made her feel important and ap-

> The classroom experience has the capability of being enhanced by a single person, the teacher.

preciated. Her teacher showed interest and reached out to her, helping my friend gain the confidence and motivation she needed to do well in the classroom. This conversation stuck with me and really got me thinking about the type of influence teachers have over their students. The fact that a college student still remembered a teacher who taught her at a very young age shows that teachers have an incredible ability to leave a meaningful and lasting impression on their students.

Through my own experiences and discussions with my peers, I have come to believe that a great teacher is one who really takes the time to get to know each and every one of his or her students. Of course, this may be a more difficult task for professors teaching at the university level, because of the large class sizes. Nevertheless, the effort a teacher puts into trying to learn more about each student never goes unnoticed. Importantly, a great teacher is also one who is able to keep students engaged during class time. This can be done through a variety of activities, including group discussions, in-class participation, and even the "discuss with your neighbor" tactic.

Although these activities keep students engaged, however, the best teachers know that bringing energy and enthusiasm to the classroom is the ultimate way to keep everyone involved. Great teachers are also those who are approachable and who listen intently when conversing with their students. Asking questions in a large classroom can be very intimidating to some students. However, when a teacher creates a comfortable environment in the classroom, this fear washes away. If a comfortable environment is not established, a student may miss out on crucial learning opportunities.

A memorable class or learning experience starts with a great teacher. Teachers are given the opportunity to create future leaders, whether they might be entrepreneurs, politicians, engineers, physicians, lawyers, or the members of any number of other professions in the community. For most students, the journey to the future begins when their teachers ask a ubiquitous question: "What do you want to be when you grow up?" This simple question fosters the development and growth of every student who walks into a classroom.

From elementary school to college, teachers are given an incredible opportunity to provide students with a memorable class experience. Caring, approachable, energetic, enthusiastic, patient, and trustworthy teachers leave a positive impression on students. The selflessness that great teachers exemplify in fulfilling the learning needs of their students is an admirable quality that should be honored by all.

BRIANNA BARREIRO

THE UNIVERSITY OF TEXAS AT EL PASO

Struggling can be an important prelude to learning.

A PROFESSOR'S INSPIRATION

EDUCATORS HAVE THE POWER to change the course of a student's life. An educator can make or break a student. I don't know about you, but to me, that sounds like the most important job out there. Without educators to teach and inspire, there would not be doctors, lawyers, police officers, etc. I know this because I was fortunate enough to meet such an educator, my chemistry professor during my first year at UT Dallas.

When I initially entered UT Dallas, I was intent on becoming a doctor. Through copious studies and extremely elevated levels of cortisol, I discovered that I did not enjoy some of the subject areas I was learning about (i.e., biochemistry and microbiology). However, I found myself enjoying my general chemistry class—words I never thought I would say. The chemistry class was so enjoyable because the chemistry professor incorporated humor, real-world scenarios, and a nonjudgmental demeanor that had every student listening. And yes, I do mean every student. I have never learned more. He earned my respect and he kept me engaged. He knew the subject backward and forward, graded fairly, and was always able to explain concepts in more than one way in a nondemeaning manner.

He was always willing to talk to his students and answer questions. I rarely saw his office door closed. He was often highly energetic and animated. I think we all know how terrible it is to listen to an educator who speaks in a monotone or reads straight from a PowerPoint presentation.

Successful educators wear many hats. They are actors, counselors, and mentors, to name a few. I discovered a passion for chemistry and wanted to teach it so that I could help eradicate the ubiquitous negative stigma associated with the field. In my four years at UT Dallas, I received the greatest amount of joy serving as a supplementary instructor and peer-led, team-learning leader to general chemistry students. My chemistry professor gave me the opportunity to experience what it is like to teach, and consequently I changed my focus from being a doctor to a teacher (much to my parents' chagrin).

> Successful educators wear many hats.

As a high school chemistry teacher, I kept my first-year chemistry class in the back of my mind. I strove to show my students that I truly cared about them and their well-being; I treated them with respect, and I never spoke to them as if they were stupid. I made sure my lessons contained humorous moments and real-world examples that would keep them focused and entertained. As a result, I am proud to say that I convinced 120 students to take my AP Chemistry class—the largest number in the entire district. I received the prestigious Teacher of the Year award for two consecutive years. My achievements in teaching led me to open a new chapter of my life, and I am currently a second-year assistant principal for a middle school in the Dallas Independent School District. I treat the students the exact same way I did when I was a teacher, which is to say the same way my chemistry professor taught me. I owe a lot to him. He showed me a career path that I am beyond passionate about.

As a chemistry student and now an educator, I have learned that if students are not comfortable with me, do not trust me, and are not intrigued by me and the subject I am teaching, they will not learn. When a great educator gains the respect of his or her students and engages them, not only will they learn, they will also be better students and people because of it. And that is a powerful thing.

MARISSA TAVALLAEE
THE UNIVERSITY OF TEXAS AT DALLAS

A great class makes students want to know more than what was taught.

GREAT STUDENTS

STAYING AMAZED: THE SECRET TO BEING A GREAT STUDENT

CURIOSITY. Keeping an open mind. Being respectful of others' ideas. Setting goals and committing to achieving them. Realizing that *real* learning is about much more than good grades. These are the threads that run through each of the following seven student essays. The question posed was deceptively simple: What makes a great student? It's noteworthy that all seven authors touched upon *skills* and *attitudes* rather than grades or content-based information. Great students are lifelong learners; in or out of school, they never tire of the thrill of "learning something new every day." As I tell my students on the first day of every semester, one must never lose the ability to be *amazed*; that is the key to staying young, having a positive impact on others, and being remembered long after you've left the building.

The traits emphasized by each of these authors also epitomize the quality of *student engagement*, a term that crops up in the teaching philosophies of so many excellent teachers. To extend Christy Hjorth's metaphor, another key ingredient in becoming/being a great student is a healthy dose of teacher engagement and passion—both for the content of the class and for the students. As Robert Bujanos notes: passion is contagious, and excellence in both learning and teaching is a two-way street. Like the yeast in a bread recipe, which needs to interact with sugar to be activated, excellent students need an equally curious, open-minded, respectful, and committed teacher to help them rise to their full potential. When that happens, when all those ingredients are present, the classroom becomes a magical mystery tour.

Engagement takes many forms, as both Pema Euden and Courtney Weston eloquently describe: coming to class prepared, listening without distraction, being respectful of everyone else in the class, asking relevant questions, contributing to discussions, and being present in the moment. All seven authors agree that the mark of a great student is not simply good grades; it is the commitment to channel the knowledge and skills gained *in* the classroom into vocations *beyond* the classroom, and the ability to carry that commitment out. Michelle Perez, Misty Martin, and Leena Berriche emphatically agree on this point: great students are inspired to use their education to find solutions to problems and help their communities, and, in turn, they inspire others to follow in their footsteps. They are role models within and outside the classroom.

Beyond academic success, great students are game changers. They think critically, problem-solve creatively, engage with others both genuinely and respectfully, and challenge themselves daily—not just to make the grade or meet the assignment requirements, but to *do something* with what they've absorbed once they have finished the class. Great students take ownership of their learning and propel their teachers to dig deeper into their teaching toolboxes. Ultimately, great students will transcend their teachers, and, frankly, that's as it should be. In my more than twenty-five-year teaching career, the students I remember most clearly are those who stumped me, who pushed me to do more research to answer their questions, who taught *me* new ways of looking at a text or solving a problem, and those whose unquenchable thirst for discovery continually rejuvenated my ability to be amazed.

DIANA DOMINGUEZ, PHD
UT SYSTEM ACADEMY OF DISTINGUISHED TEACHERS
THE UNIVERSITY OF TEXAS RIO GRANDE VALLEY

GRADES ARE NOT THE ONLY MEASURE

IF YOU ASK SOMEONE what makes a great student, I am positive that the answer would include something along the lines of "good grades and a high GPA." While grades and GPA certainly play a large role in academic success, we cannot limit the definition of a great student to his or her academic achievements. Instead, there are many qualities that great students possess aside from their academic ability.

The most important qualities of great students, in my opinion, include dedication, perseverance, a desire to learn, active involve-

> To be great, a student has to *want* to be great.

ment in community, and academic achievement. Great students are goal-setters with high ambitions. They use hard work and dedication in order to reach and maintain their goals, which shows how committed they can be. However, to be great, a student has to *want* to be great and has to actively motivate himself or herself to reach those goals and persevere. Many students are happy to settle for mediocre grades, but why not try harder? If you are going to be anything, why not try to be the best at it?

To be a great student does not mean that you are necessarily the smartest in the class; instead, it means you are willing to try your best at everything you put your mind to. A great student should have an insatiable appetite for knowledge, constantly craving a greater understanding of the chosen area of interest. These students are proud of the knowledge they possess, but they do not fear asking questions when unsure or in need of clarification. Being an active member of society is particularly important because it shows a student's selflessness and desire to help others. It allows the student to be a well-rounded individual. Great students are the ones who care deeply and are willing to help others. Academic success still tends to be the deal-breaker in determining if a student is *great*. But while grades can be a good indicator, they should not be the only measurement of success. We should instead incorporate the other qualities mentioned previously.

One of the reasons I feel I am a great student is that I actively encourage myself to be my very best. Academic achievement is extremely important to me because a good foundation in my undergraduate career will set me up for success in my professional career. I strive to understand my own limitations in terms of how I learn, and I always make sure to study and learn concepts in my own learning style. This strategy allows me to fully grasp the material. Afterward, I strive to apply the newly learned material by helping others learn. Within my major, we face many difficult courses, and persevering through them has helped to build my resilience. I have grown more and more to appreciate my peers and professors for their never-ending help.

Where there are great students, there are also bad students. I would consider a student to be *bad* if he or she does not care about grades or the future. As young adults, we need to be cautious and remember that (as in physics) every action has a reaction. If we choose to slack off now, where does that put us in the future? It is important to plan now and set ourselves up for success. Remember this quote from the famed UCLA coach John Wooden: "If you don't have time to do it right, when will you have time to do it over?" Understand that the more you give to your academic career, the more you will gain in the long run.

All students have the potential to be great students! It is never too late to start focusing on your academic career and becoming a great student. It simply takes motivation, hard work, and perseverance. Remember also that even if your GPA is not the highest, you are still worthy of being great!

MISTY MARTIN

THE UNIVERSITY OF TEXAS AT ARLINGTON

What will students remember about
your class in twenty years?

CHARACTERISTICS OF
AN EXCELLENT STUDENT

THE TERM "STUDENT" might just be a seven-letter word, but it is one that has immense meaning. It represents the vast majority of people, given that most people have been students at some point in their lives. Of course, students come to class with a wide variety of personalities, perspectives, and preferences. In my opinion, a great student is one who is respectful, hardworking, and willing to learn new things.

For a person to willingly learn from another person, he or she should have respect for the teacher. Respect does not mean blindly following instruction. It means hav-

> A great student is one who is respectful, hardworking, and willing to learn new things.

ing the patience to listen to the teacher and understanding that the teacher has the best interest of the student at heart. A great student also respects that the teacher is human and can make mistakes. In such instances, a great student can explain his or her approach to the problem without getting upset.

Respect, however, is not just for the teacher. A great student has respect for his or her fellow classmates as well.

He or she has an open mind when discussing answers or studying with classmates. A respectful student is patient and able to explain his or her answers to others, and also listens to others when they do the same. It is important to respect the personal space of teachers and classmates, and to respect the learning environment, whether it is a small classroom or the whole university.

Determination and hard work are required for anyone to achieve his or her goals. For a student to excel in any class, these qualities are indispensable. A good student listens in class and usually hands in assignments on time, but a great student takes the time to study and work on problems he or she doesn't yet feel comfortable with. If the student doesn't get it even after a few tries, giving up is not an option. Reading reference books, watching tutorials, and going to the professor or teaching assistant for help are all in a great student's repertoire.

Most important of all, a great student should have the curiosity and willingness to learn new things. Whatever the subject is, the lesson becomes interesting and homework is not a burden if a student takes a real interest. A great student looks forward to class each day, excited to learn something new. He or she goes beyond what is taught in class and learns much more than expected. Despite the saying "Curiosity killed the cat," I believe that having a curious mind both inside and outside of school develops our minds and makes us better students. Hence, every great student must have an eagerness to learn new things.

Respect, hard work, and curiosity are what make a great student. Students and teachers are not just found in school or college. Our friends, family members, or even strangers can be our teachers at times. Whether we are teachers or students, we should each strive to be our best versions of ourselves.

PEMA EUDEN
THE UNIVERSITY OF TEXAS AT EL PASO

Teaching is like a gas.
It takes up all available space.

RECIPE FOR A GREAT STUDENT

INGREDIENTS
- Motivation
- Organization
- Hard work
- Materials

DIRECTIONS

Find Your Motivation: The most important factor in becoming a great student is having an internal drive to be successful. This is what will influence your success the most. Whether your goal is working toward a long-term career option or just completing a simple assignment, you must be able to motivate yourself to pursue the goal until you reach it. Create goals that you can achieve. Without goals, it becomes easy to lose focus during the difficult times you will inevitably encounter while getting an education.

> Without goals, it becomes easy to lose focus during the difficult times you will inevitably encounter while getting an education.

Create an Organizational System: Having an organizational system is a simple way to remind yourself of educational and life events. Planners, physical or digital, no matter how in-depth or plain, are essential. Without a system, due dates and assignments may be forgotten in the semester among the stresses of life. The good thing about planners is that they can be complex and detailed or provide just the essentials. Be sure to experiment with different organizational systems to find the best way for you to be successful.

Work for Your Goal: Hard work is an essential component to becoming a great student. Make a plan for your life that incorporates your goals so that you can realistically achieve them. This element is the difference between a smart student and an intelligent student.

Gather Your Materials: Go to class! It is essential for you to hear your professors' explanations and to take notes so that you will remember concepts. Outside of class, talk to your professors, review your class notes, read your book for any clarifications, and then rewrite your notes in a way that will help you study them. Even though it's tempting to skip those 8:00 a.m. classes, persevere and remember you are studying to achieve your goals.

CHRISTY HJORTH
THE UNIVERSITY OF TEXAS AT TYLER

*How has your teaching changed
since the first time you taught?*

DETERMINING WHAT MAKES
A GOOD STUDENT:
A GOOD PERSON

AS A TEACHER, one sees every type of individual in the classroom setting. There will be a student who sits in the front and attends every lecture, a student who sits in the back for every lecture, and then a student who only shows up for a test. While students who only attend for a test may come off as *bad* students, they may have other life circumstances working against them. Background will play a key role in the quality of students, as everyone faces different situations in life. How, then, is it possible to determine whether a student is *good*, and what factors play a role?

While one student might come to every lecture and sit in the front, he or she may sit quietly and never ask a question. A student who sits in the back may make it a point to contact their teacher and ask questions as necessary. Such students may be kind and respectful and may notify teachers of their situations. It would be ideal if everyone enjoyed the subject matter, but this will not always be the case. There is a long list of core classes for each student to take, and the science major may not jump for joy on the way to a history

> Background will play a key role in the quality of students, as everyone faces different situations in life.

class. Because it is not what that student chose as a major, it's not of interest. The difference between the student who loves the class and the one who couldn't care less should not be apparent to the professor, however. A science major can show interest in learning the material regardless of his or her major or personal interests. That is one thing that determines whether the student is a good student.

It is possible that even a good student, one who has chosen the subject matter as a major, can have trouble making it to class, but may still be sure to get notes from a peer and read the material. This student may struggle with the challenges that come with university-level work, but may still be putting forth effort to succeed in the class and maintain decent grades. The ones who come and don't pay attention—whether they spend class time searching for something on the web, texting their friends, or playing a game—may be considered *bad* students. There are places for them to take part in these activities, and a classroom is not one of them. It's distracting to peers as well as disrespectful to the professor.

Everyone has a different background and a different motivation for being there, but it's the work ethic they bring into the classroom that makes the difference. The ones who sit behind the desk and listen to the lecture without distraction, who read the material and are ready for questions, and who put in the work and effort to engage in the material, regardless of their personal interest level— these are the students who stand out and demonstrate a clear line between good students and bad ones. Those who show up and present themselves as mature adults, who are respectful of the time of those around them, will make a far greater impact than the others. Those who do not want to waste their time by sitting idly, but are present in the moment, are the ones who will make a difference in society, and who will change the future after walking across the stage on graduation day.

COURTNEY WESTON
THE UNIVERSITY OF TEXAS AT ARLINGTON

The best class is one in which students keep learning long after it's over.

SHAPING THE FUTURE

A SIMPLISTIC EXPLANATION might say that a great student is someone who pays attention, contributes to lectures, takes good notes, gets good grades, and assists his or her classmates. I believe that, although these qualities are essential and provide the foundation for who will become a great student, further consideration is needed to pin down the necessary qualities.

What then is the essence of a great student? To be sure, a great student is a leader, a mentor, and a public servant, someone who shares his or her educational experiences to encourage others in intellectual pursuits. A great student is inspired to use education to find solutions to existing problems within the community while inspiring others to do the same. Great students develop a dedication to personal enrichment through lifelong education with a commitment to their careers, families, and communities.

Through their actions, great students convey how education has helped them by helping others. One way this is accomplished is by continually refining one's skill set, then sharing this knowledge and expertise through mentoring. A student who does this can teach what he or she knows while understanding the mentee's capabilities.

Another mark of a great student is the ability to be innovative in promoting the quality of life in the community. To do this, it is important to be able to relate to a diverse group of people, including stakeholders, and influence them to recognize and address social challenges.

Great students learn to examine issues critically, can think outside the box, and avoid the pitfalls of groupthink. As these students evolve, they become disciplined in self-awareness and can understand the cultural attributes of others. They can then apply this understanding toward improving the quality of life and growth of the community as a whole. A great student is one who is not happy just to attain good marks or earn a diploma, because he or she understands that this alone does not ensure a prosperous existence.

> Great students learn to examine issues critically, can think outside the box, and avoid the pitfalls of groupthink.

Anyone who is dedicated to avoiding the biases formed by culture has the potential to be a great student. Ultimately, it takes an individual who is not hindered by conventional structures and who uses his or her education to engage people in positive ways to shape the future for a better tomorrow.

MICHELLE PEREZ

THE UNIVERSITY OF TEXAS AT EL PASO

Learning to think can be uncomfortable.

STRIVING FOR EXCELLENCE

We need to internalize this idea of excellence. Not many folks spend a lot of time trying to be excellent.

—BARACK OBAMA

TO EXCEL IS to be outstanding, and that should be something everybody strives for. That drive for excellence is especially critical in the classroom, because this sets the foundation for students to become successful and involved in the world after they leave school. But what is excellence in the classroom exactly? From my experience as a student, I'd like to offer some examples.

In my opinion, teachers have the most important job in the educational system. They are at the core of the learning process. The teachers who have had the most positive impact on me are the ones who have gone above and beyond the basic requirements. Personally, I have found that when teachers show passion for the subject they teach, as well as for their students, I try harder than I normally would because I don't want to disappoint them, and I wonder what makes them so passionate. I also tend to learn more with an instructor who knows when to give direction and when to let the students take the initiative and work it out for themselves. Also, when the teacher is genuine, I feel like that really creates an environment that fosters learning and curiosity.

Expanding on the teaching environment, it's very important that students feel safe enough to contribute. Understandably, the teacher is supposed to give instruction most of the time, but it's been my experience that lots of opportunities for student participation make the difference between an *okay* class

> It's very important that students feel safe enough to contribute.

and an *excellent* class. This is how ideas and lessons really leave their mark on students. The way this is achieved is by first establishing trust and promoting confidence in us. A way I have seen this work well is to start the semester off by asking students to speak about something they know about, whether it's just their names and a little something about themselves or reading a short excerpt of something they really like. This approach works because the student is not wrong and will not feel too embarrassed to speak up at the next opportunity. Group activities also work very well to establish connections among students, as they give us a valid reason to communicate freely with each other.

Often, just a simple effort put forward by the student makes all the difference between passing or failing and understanding or existing in ignorance. Without effort, scholars cannot achieve academic greatness of any sort. An excellent student is one who has an insatiable thirst for knowledge and an ability to tackle whatever obstacle is in the way, and we all know that obstacles will arise. Students must put aside all their biases and preconceived notions of an area of study and approach it with an open mind.

They must find answers that really mean something and apply them to the world around them. An excellent student has the discipline to adhere to a strict schedule of scholarly inquiry, even if this means following the rules of the institution. Personally, I hate having to conform to a list of rules, especially when they do not seem necessary to me, but sometimes it's what I must do to achieve my goals.

Effort needs to be made on both sides of the teacher/student relationship to really make a difference. This is the most basic of all the aspects of a great student, but it's also the most important one. It's the basis of the whole concept, and without a base nothing can stand.

ROBERT BUJANOS
THE UNIVERSITY OF TEXAS RIO GRANDE VALLEY

Is your class a monologue or a dialogue?

HOW LEARNING FLOURISHES

I ASKED MY DAD for a laptop when I was fourteen years old. My excuse was that I *needed* one to be a successful student. My father quickly dismissed me: "I studied in the light of an oil lamp. If you want to study, you will study." Although I rolled my eyes at the expected when-I-was-a-boy response of my Tunisian, immigrant father, his message has inspired my understanding of what constitutes a successful student. My father responded in the way he did because he knew that I *wanted* to learn, and that ultimately, nothing he could do could change that. If a student has a desire to learn and to discover, no excuse will stand in her way.

Recently, I watched a TED Talk by Angela Lee Duckworth. In this lecture, Duckworth set out to define the *determining factor of student success*. She came to the conclusion that it's not the "naturally smart" students who will be the most successful—rather, it's the students with what she calls "grit." A student with grit is one who has a growth mindset. Instead of saying, "This subject is too hard, so I'm probably not going to pass," these students are the ones who will say, "This subject is difficult, so I am going to set aside more time to understand it better."

For the past three years, I have been a part-time tutor in my university's Student Success Center. I tutored calculus before transitioning to tutoring organic chemistry. Calculus was a subject I instantly grasped; organic chemistry was not, which is why I decided to tutor it. It is a subject that is traditionally very daunting to most students. I didn't decide to tutor it because I knew everything about the subject, but because I wanted other students to see that a growth mindset is all it takes to succeed at it. At the start of each semester, eight students sign up to meet in a group with me each week for the rest of the course.

The first thing I always ask them is, "What have you heard about this class?"

I get a plethora of nervous responses. They already typically have preconceived notions that it is an insurmountable subject. I advise them to dispel those ideas before attempting to learn the course material. I tell them how this young student didn't perform well on her first exam because she went into the course thinking it was impossible. I tell them how that drove her to even spend all her Friday nights in review sessions. I tell them how the time and effort she threw into understanding the material gave her a newfound appreciation for it. That young student was, of course, me.

The most effective instructors are those whose relatability makes them feel accessible to me. One of my instructors demonstrated this when he told the class, "As a student, I couldn't hold an attention span for more than thirty minutes in lectures." He made his classes discussion based, realizing that students responded better to that format. When I admit to my students at the Success Center that I struggled with the concepts I am now tutoring, they begin to understand that learning isn't always about having natural talent; it's about making an effort and having endurance in the endeavor. An instructor willing to admit that he may not have the best attention span taught me the importance of being relatable and honest. Learning depends on a relentless desire to learn and the mindset of staying motivated in the face of academic adversity, and the real and relatable communication of an instructor can help that motivation flourish.

LEENA BERRICHE
THE UNIVERSITY OF TEXAS AT DALLAS

A caring professor understands that his or her course is only part of a student's academic and off-campus life.

HEALTHY MINDS,
HEALTHY STUDENTS

MAKING MENTAL HEALTH A PRIORITY

PURSUING A COLLEGE DEGREE can be a stressful endeavor. The application process, the complex registration and financial aid processes, the ever-changing slate of courses, and figuring out how to pay for the opportunity to meet all of these challenges can feel overwhelming. In their joint essay, students Melina Acosta and Saifa Pirani discuss stress and mental illness on college campuses. According to Activeminds, a national nonprofit focused on college student mental health, almost one-third of college students report having felt so depressed that they had trouble functioning. Eighty percent say they have felt overwhelmed by what they had to do, and 45 percent said they have felt things were hopeless. In their respective essays, Bianca Hsieh gives a compelling account of how her effort to be a model student caused her emotional and academic stress, Jessica Goodwin discusses the challenges of continuing her studies while coping with major depressive disorder, and Tyler Klein talks about how the pressures experienced by student athletes can negatively impact their performance and well-being.

This is not to say that all distressed students are experiencing full-blown clinical depression or anxiety, although the numbers of students meeting criteria for these disorders are on the rise. But experiencing even some of the symptoms of depression and anxiety—which include sadness, helplessness, lack of motivation, rumination, difficulty concentrating, and sleep disturbances—are associated with reduced GPA and failure to complete college. Most disturbingly, over 1,000 college students commit suicide in the United States every year. Further complicating the picture is the fact that eating disorders, as well as conditions such as bipolar disorder and schizophrenia, often emerge in young adulthood, and may catch students and their families off-guard as they try to determine why a student seems to be changing or struggling. Students do have different levels of resilience and strategies for coping with stress, but typical student behaviors, including poor diet, poor sleep and exercise patterns, and substance abuse issues, can also trigger or exacerbate any of these mental health issues.

Of course, students don't exist in a vacuum while attending college. Whether they live at home, in the dorms, or off campus, they usually continue to have contact with their families and spend time with friends and fellow classmates. In many cases they also have an extensive social media presence, although such attenuated contacts can be stressful in themselves. Students also interact with a wide variety of people while attending school, from housing administrative staff to advisers to professors. However, not all of these individuals are trained to recognize or respond to signs of mental distress. Family members are often afraid to admit that someone has a mental illness, or just hope the problem will go away on its own. Staff members and faculty fear that they will say something that makes the situation worse, or that alienates the student, and students hide their distress for fear of embarrassment.

The solution, of course, is for all of us to stop ignoring the problem and face it head on. The onus is on educators, students, and families alike to educate ourselves on how to recognize and respond to mental distress, and to become familiar with the resources available to help people in distress. A number of reliable sources of information regarding mental illness and suicide prevention can be found online. There are also training courses in topics such as Psychological First Aid that teach laypeople how to help those in acute distress. In addition, most universities have a variety of resources available for students in distress. These include counseling services, which are typically covered by student fees; ombudsman offices that can help students with everything from mental health problems to obtaining emergency loans; behavioral intervention teams that can mobilize resources to help students who are a possible risk to themselves or others; and offices that can respond to specific student needs, including disability services, veteran services, and equal opportunity services. As the essay by Michael Camele indicates, faculty are in a unique position to make students aware of campus support systems.

However, none of these resources are helpful if students and the people who care about them fail to understand why students are distressed or to encourage students to seek help. Stigmas recede when confronted, and mental health issues can be addressed with the appropriate treatment.

College campuses are communities in their own right with their own ambience, culture, and shared goals, but communities can only function as well as their members. Making mental health a priority should be everyone's goal.

MARY MCNAUGHTON-CASSILL, PHD
UT SYSTEM ACADEMY OF DISTINGUISHED TEACHERS
THE UNIVERSITY OF TEXAS AT SAN ANTONIO

HOW TO HELP

"I AM AT MY MENTAL LIMIT and need help getting through this semester."

Many college students have uttered some variant of this statement, whether exasperatedly to themselves or dejectedly to an instructor. The process of admitting that one needs help can be daunting, considering how professors may react.

As psychology students, perhaps it is natural that we are cognizant of our mental health. Our professors lecture about stress and coping frequently. When we share with them our mental health struggles, they collaborate with us to find a solution, never questioning the legitimacy of our concerns.

Students in other majors have different experiences. Many would never consider telling their closest friends about their mental health concerns, let alone their instructors, for fear of being stigmatized. Maybe the instructor would think of them differently. Maybe the instructor would not empathize. Maybe the instructor would be made uncomfortable. Maybe the student's thinking would be confirmed—maybe their mental health is just an excuse for their inability to handle the workload.

Epidemiological studies indicate that 20–25 percent of Americans have a diagnosable mental illness. Common sense tells us that 100 percent of people have mental health issues. Dealing with student mental health concerns should not be reserved for faculty from the psychology and counseling departments. Mental health affects us all.

How can faculty members be sensitive to the mental health needs of their students? Certainly, instructors are not expected to behave as therapists for struggling students. Nor are they expected to know how to say all the right things and be able to help these students alone. We offer two pieces of advice for faculty to become more attuned to student mental health.

First, instructors can be mindful of the language they use in class. There are instructors who attribute their well-organized content on Blackboard Learn to their "OCD tendencies," or who joke about their exams or assignments

> How can an educational institution improve if it does not view the mental well-being of its students as a serious issue?

causing students PTSD. Jokes can lighten up the mood and capture student interest, but this should not be at the expense of making light of mental illnesses like panic attacks, obsessive-compulsive disorder (OCD), depression, posttraumatic stress disorder (PTSD), or even suicide. Not only do these statements discourage students who live with these conditions from reaching out to their instructors for help, but they also reinforce the societal stigma surrounding mental health and illness. How can an educational institution expect to improve academic performance, retention rates, and graduation rates if it does not view the mental well-being of its students as a serious issue?

When a student does share his mental health struggles with a faculty member, it may be tempting for the instructor to offer advice or anecdotes to assuage the student's distress. However, it is even simpler to first validate the student's feelings with statements like, "I believe you," "I cannot imagine how difficult this must be for you," or even simply, "Thank you for feeling comfortable enough to share this with me." From there, the instructor can refer the student to campus counseling services for further evaluation and potential treatment. Depending on the student's preference and the severity of the situation, instructors can provide the student with the contact information and location of counseling services or can directly contact counseling services on behalf of the student. Some instructors may even take it upon themselves to walk with the student to counseling services. Connecting the student to the right resources, even if you do not know exactly what to say, is all it takes to help a student in distress. You never know when you may be saving a life.

MELINA ACOSTA AND SAIFA PIRANI
THE UNIVERSITY OF TEXAS AT SAN ANTONIO

Some classes are better when the teacher doesn't have all the right answers.

RECOGNIZING STUDENTS IN NEED

TODAY MARKS a completed year and a half of my collegiate experience at the University of Texas at Austin. When I accepted my admission to the university and selected Plan II and Business Honors, I was prepared for an intellectual challenge. However, these past few months have called into question something more than academics: my understanding of myself.

I explored numerous opportunities my first year and managed to survive relatively unscathed. Determined to make the most out of my sophomore year, I signed up for more interesting but demanding classes and landed leadership positions in various organizations. I was ready to take on the year. However, my grades began to slip, my commitments were spread thin, and my mental health deteriorated. As I was not able to take care of myself mentally and emotionally, the consequences began to manifest physically. I was having a difficult time staying awake in classes, if I even made it to them at all. I was becoming more reluctant to speak up in my discussions, an attribute that hurt me in classes that graded based on participation. I was a kid succumbing to the pressures of needing to ace all my classes, have a Google/Facebook/Apple internship lined up for the summer, and be social all at the same time.

During this time, a professor from one of my core classes reached out to me because she had noticed there was a deterioration of my behavior during her class. She asked me to come to see her during office hours, and, relieved to have someone to talk to, I confided in her about all my anxieties and worries. Throughout the remainder of the semester, this professor would keep up with me, occasionally checking in on how I was doing. I eventually sought out a counselor, based on her recommendation, and I have been going to these appointments consistently.

Upon reflection, I have come to understand that the difference between a great teacher and a bad teacher is not necessarily a function of academic merit, tenure, or number of publications. Rather, the difference, at least for me, is the ability to recognize when a student, a human being, needs help, especially in an environment as fluid as college life. As a student in two honors programs, I was told that all the professors in my honors classes were exceptional and at the tops of their fields. Though I did not doubt this, these professors would also pile on exorbitant amounts of reading and assignments and expect an incredibly short turnaround time, causing me and many of my classmates to become burned out in the process. The professor from that core course, however, even though she was teaching a class with many more students than were in my honors courses, recognized that her

> The difference between a great teacher and a bad teacher is the ability to recognize when a student, a human being, needs help.

students were only human and structured her class accordingly. Many of the students may have thought this was an "easy class," but if anything, this structure and her decision to reach out probably saved my life.

I came to the university determined to create a new persona for myself. I rushed the Greek system in hopes of joining a sorority. I socialized and went out on the weekends, even though I would have preferred to stay in and read a new book. I began to prioritize a set of values that were not in line with those of the girl who was so captivated with learning that she applied to Plan II to continue her intellectual journey. I felt purposeless and lost in a sea of 51,000 other students.

As my sophomore year progressed, I didn't end up in a sorority, and sometimes I did opt to stay in rather than going out. With the help of my professor and now my counselor, I am aiming to shape a new perspective focused on internal rather than external validation. I am coming to terms with my shortcomings and celebrating my strengths as I try to figure out my identity at UT Austin with a little help from great teachers.

BIANCA HSIEH
THE UNIVERSITY OF TEXAS AT AUSTIN

The professor shouldn't be the only teacher in the room.

WHAT MAKES A STUDENT
FAIL OR STRUGGLE?

MY STRUGGLE AS A STUDENT began when I was diag-
nosed with major depressive disorder and premenstrual
dysphoric disorder (PMDD) last year. It actually began before that, but after my first semester at UT Dallas it became relentless. I graduated from Kilgore College with
Presidential Honors in 2014 with an associate degree in
behavioral science. I also received Academic Recognition
certificates in excellence, Phi Theta Kappa awards, and
Sigma Kappa Delta awards. I'm not trying to toot my own
horn. I'm just providing some background about my life
before the depression hit me.

I had struggled little in school previously. In fact, as an
older student I was surpassing my wildest dreams. After
moving to Dallas, I went through some significant stress,
however, and it's been a constant struggle ever since. Bat-
tling depression is one of the most challenging things I've
ever experienced. I have days where I will get my assignments in on time and do what is expected of me. Then I
will have days, even weeks, where I don't get out of bed,
or turn on a light or a television, much less go to class. I
take my child to school, get back in bed, get up to make
him dinner, and get back in bed. It's been a struggle to

push through, but I have. This is my fourth semester here. I did great during my first semester. The spring and summer semesters of 2016 hit me hard, but I earned Cs. Then in the fall of 2017, I got all As. I am now doing okay on my exams, but depression is practically taking over my world. Today, I feel fantastic, and many days I feel unstoppable. Then the episodes begin to hit me all over again.

As a psychology major, I feel that I should be able to help myself, but I know that is not possible. I am looking into counseling here at UT Dallas and hopefully can get some assistance. I feel fortunate not to have failed, yet the struggle continues. My professors have been extremely understanding, and I know that I can bring myself through these dark times.

As a student, major stressors are the main reason I am struggling. I truly believe that. I understand that classes are demanding and have many challenges, and I usually take these challenges head on . . . until the depression hits again like a ton of bricks. I suppose I am being a bit redundant, but I remember my family saying, "Just go to the gym," or "Snap out of it," or "Depression isn't real. It's all in your head. Get over it." I am fortunate to have taken enough psychology classes to know that it's not just something you can completely snap out of. It's not possible, and if left unattended, it can take over your life. Each day, it's a gamble. Am I going to be able to get out of bed? I hate that it has become this bad, but it has, and I have to tackle this head on. I read in my sociology book that 25 percent of all college students experience burnout, so I try not to be too hard on myself. I take it day by day. I'm ready to feel 100 percent again.

Right now, I have all Bs and a C. I have done this without any books because I could not afford them, yet another stressor. But I don't let it stop me. Depression will not get the better of me. The value that I place on my education is immeasurable. I hope for my depression to release its claws, but no matter what, I will continue to persevere.

JESSICA GOODWIN
THE UNIVERSITY OF TEXAS AT DALLAS

*The best class is one in which
the teacher barely talks.*

HELPING STUDENTS
OVERCOME SELF-DOUBT

UNIVERSITY LIFE AFFORDS FREEDOMS to students in their academic careers that they may not have experienced prior to attending college. There is less adult supervision, class assignments become complex, and students are encouraged to take active roles in their education. However, these newfound freedoms also bring uncertainty.

Prior to college, there are many rules that students follow like a checklist, ensuring they are acting as expected. However, upon entering college, the rules become less explicit, and students wonder if they are doing the right thing—or, conversely, if they are failing to meet expectations. As a result, students may develop self-doubt or unreasonable expectations. This may lead to a lack of quiet self-confidence in their abilities—the very trait teachers want to develop and nurture in their students. While students can seek feedback or guidance from their peers, oftentimes this is perceived as fishing for compliments. How might teachers help students overcome their self-doubts and develop confidence in their early years in college?

Professors should stress their availability and willingness to socialize with students—this can range from making small talk with students before class to providing specific examples of the kind of help they can offer during office hours, or requiring casual out-of-class meetings to discuss a student's progress in the course. Even something as simple as informing students about how one prefers to be contacted—for example, via email—can help students feel more comfortable about connecting with their professors. Additionally, professors should consider using precision and directness when outlining course and assignment guidelines. For example, providing students with detailed rubrics and examples of student work along with the grade each earned can remove some of the guesswork—and stress—for students.

Along with these measures, it is important for students to know they are supported—either by their professors or through available counseling services on campus. While students must know when to seek out these programs, professors can help make students more aware of these campus services. As a passive measure, these services could be mentioned in course syllabi. As an active measure, professors—through regular socializing with students in and out of the classroom—can try to be aware of their students' mental health and take action as needed.

> It is important for students to know they are supported.

During my own time at the University of Texas at Arlington, I have benefited immensely from friendships with a handful of supportive professors. While my professors were all supportive academically—encouraging students to take active roles in learning, showing enthusiasm for ideas in class discussion, and so on—it has been the professors who took on a more social relationship who have been the most beneficial to me as a student. For example, I once had a professor who, after class, would eagerly approach me to discuss television shows, movies, books, and music. These casual chats were great—instead of thinking of this professor as an all-powerful grade-giver or viewing the class as an excruciating academic exercise, I became eager to attend class and tackle course assignments. It didn't feel like I was attending class at all—instead, I was spending an hour with a friend who just happened to know more about a subject I was interested in than I did. Similarly, with professors who have taken the time to get to know me, I have felt comfortable seeking life advice and discussing my anxieties. They have made me feel more supported as an individual both in and out of the classroom. Were it not for these friendships, I likely would never have finished my degree. Now, thanks to these professors, I can't imagine my newfound eagerness for learning ever going away.

MICHAEL CAMELE
THE UNIVERSITY OF TEXAS AT ARLINGTON

Teaching is about connections.

PERSPECTIVES FROM A
FORMER STUDENT ATHLETE

TEACHING EVALUATIONS clearly indicate that students value different things from their instructors based on their prior educational experiences, personalities, and academic goals. However, for some students, the academic portion of their college experience is only part of their job. At Division I schools, student athletes are expected to perform well in class while devoting significant amounts of their time and energy to their sport. Although NCAA regulations cap organized sports participation at twenty hours per week, in reality the commitment is often higher.

Travel time, independent practice and exercise, injury rehabilitation/avoidance efforts, mental preparation and training, and team building and volunteer activities all take their toll. Athletes also experience dramatic schedule changes when their sport is in-season and sometimes feel isolated from the larger campus community because of their sport commitments. Unfortunately, injuries are also common among student athletes and can have a negative impact on their athletic and academic success as well as their mental health.

While athletes should not expect preferential treatment, there are things faculty can do to promote their success both in and out of the classroom. The following are practices that I recommend based on my personal experience and academic training:

1. Avoid judging current students on the basis of previous experiences and prejudice. Intra-group differences always exist, and stereotyping students on the basis of their appearance or sport of choice does them a disservice.

2. Ask for details if the student or coach does not supply relevant information regarding practice and game schedules and student obligations.

3. Help students manage their time effectively by explaining and providing written documentation regarding the demands of the course and your policy for rearranging assignments and exams.

4. Show you care about your students' academic performance by maintaining professional but open lines of communication, showing respect for students, and expecting them to be accountable for their performance.

5. Develop a classroom culture that is accepting and inclusive by making students from all backgrounds converse with other students to create a climate of collaboration. This will set the stage for all students to create diverse social networks within your classroom.

6. Ask student athletes to relate their specific experiences to the content of the class as a means of reinforcing their abilities as athletes and students.

Of course, student athletes also vary along a continuum of academic orientation, ranging from the belief that college sports are a stepping stone to a professional sports career to the belief that participating in athletics should have no impact on academic performance. Flexibility, personal interest, respect, understanding, and a small amount of effort on the part of instructors can help student athletes develop confidence in their academic abilities as well as their athletic skills. As a result, the classroom, which for many is seen as a means to an athletic end, can become a valued playing field as well.

> A small amount of effort on the part of instructors can help student athletes develop confidence.

TYLER KLEIN

THE UNIVERSITY OF TEXAS AT SAN ANTONIO

Teaching a subject is the best way to learn it.

STUDENTS OF ANY AGE

THE DIVERSITY INDEX IS OLD HAT:
IT NEEDS MORE OLD HATS

"LET'S WASTE COLLEGE ON THE OLD" was the headline of an op-ed piece in the *New York Times* on October 31, 2017. In the essay, Paul Glastris, editor-in-chief of the *Washington Monthly*, makes convincing arguments for recruiting more students twenty-five and older to universities.

At least five of the students contributing to this book would need little convincing. They know that, especially at public universities, having "middle-aged" students in the classroom is becoming the "new normal," to quote one of the students, Holly McDonald, UT El Paso. Holly and the others emphasize that, in her words, these students bring "experience and knowledge" that create a "richer learning experience."

The experience/knowledge contribution is obvious. What I especially appreciated about the students' viewpoints is that they went beyond the obvious to suggest how older students can become role models, and how they can expand concepts of "university learning" to include spaces as large as a factory and as small as a three-bedroom home.

In her definition of a model student, Victoria Inman-Hinesly, UT Permian Basin, a young student, features being "prepared" and "do[ing] their work" for all students.

However, she singles out older students for another quality: "They want to be there." Unlike some of her eighteen-to twenty-two-year-old classmates who weren't sure why they were in college or if college was worth the effort, the middle-aged students knew why they were there and had made difficult life decisions to advance toward those goals. Cory Knight, UT San Antonio, and Julieta Scalo, UT Austin, add that with maturity comes different attitudes about studying. When he was young, Cory blamed teachers for his poor grades. When he developed more personal responsibility about his performance, he became an honors student and went on to graduate school. For Julieta, maturity transformed studying from being a "chore" into an "adventure" that led to a PhD. Of course, all older students aren't model students, but I can understand why Victoria could look up to them for inspiration as models of hard workers—work that was personally meaningful, goal-oriented, and full of adventure.

Edward Gunderson, UT El Paso, and Holly emphasize how older students can expand the concepts of "classroom" and "teacher." Edward returned to college after serving in Afghanistan. In his attempt to define great teachers, he ventures far beyond college classrooms to consider qualities demonstrated by his father, his Taekwondo instructor, and an instructor who presented company managers as important teachers. The latter concept of teaching has inspired Edward to find ways to instruct present and future employees to perform well. For him, a factory or a business complex can turn into an enlarged classroom.

Holly's expanded classroom was much smaller but more accessible: it was her domestic space. She defines herself as a "middle-aged student," an "an average mom." Typically, students complain about conflicts between university and family responsibilities. In Holly's case, her return to school turned her family into a cooperative learning environment. Instead of bringing snacks to her eight-year-old to keep her study times energized, her daughter brought Holly snacks when her mom studied. Holly's seventeen-year-old left (at least temporarily) his social media devices and became a study buddy who discussed his dual credit courses, as well as his and his mom's mutual educational goals. Holly's husband took over many household duties. Of course, not all families respond this way, but Holly's experience demonstrates how a mother's return to college can transform a household. That's another type of model Holly could share with her younger classmates.

Holly, Victoria, Cory, Julieta, and Edward make strong cases for revising the way educational think tanks typically define "Diversity Indexes." Those numbers need to highlight age diversity, and students and parents mulling over college choices would do well to make age diversity a crucial factor in their decisions.

KENNETH ROEMER, PhD
UT SYSTEM ACADEMY OF DISTINGUISHED TEACHERS
THE UNIVERSITY OF TEXAS AT ARLINGTON

THE NEW NORMAL

I FIRMLY BELIEVE a good support system can make any student successful, and I think I am a good example of this. I'm a forty-something UTEP Connect student. I used to think I wasn't your typical college student, but I'm beginning to think that middle-aged students are the new normal! I'm a wife, a mother of two kids, and a full-time employee. When I was younger, I had little to no support system for school; to attest to that, I started and stopped college multiple times in my teens and twenties. I went back to school in my thirties and received my associate degree from Brookhaven College. I stopped school for a while again and am now back as a full-time student. I have found that returning to college later in life has given me a different focus than I had previously. I have experience and knowledge that I didn't have in my twenties, so I feel like I am having a richer learning experience than ever before.

My near-term goal is to obtain my bachelor's degree in multidisciplinary studies online. I took twelve hours in the fall semester (all As!) and am enrolled for an-

> I have found that returning to college later in life has given me a different focus than I had previously.

other fifteen hours this spring. My family is very supportive of my endeavors. My eight-year-old daughter likes to snack while she is doing her homework, so she always makes sure I'm well stocked with snacks and drinks while I'm studying. My seventeen-year-old son is, well, a seventeen-year-old. He spends more time in his room and on his devices than he does with us, but we have had multiple conversations about schooling and the importance of an advanced education. He's enrolled in dual credit courses, so he understands the struggle of working on your college education while trying to have a life outside of textbooks. My husband is my biggest cheerleader and has taken on the lion's share of kid and house duties to make sure I achieve my educational goals. He also pays me the household rate for As—five dollars each, thank you very much.

My manager is also very supportive of my educational goals, frequently checking in to see what he can do to keep me motivated. We have discussed obtaining a degree as the impetus for a promotion, so I keep this in mind during those moments when the stresses of work, parenting, and school start to collide. The knowledge that obtaining a degree will help advance my career in the clinical research industry is one thing that propels me forward. I have worked in clinical operations in the pharmaceutical arena for almost twenty years, but, without a degree, had found myself to be maxed out as far as career advancement is concerned. I am no longer complacent. I want my career to have more forward momentum, and this degree will help propel me in that direction.

I am just an average mom attempting to reach a goal that I have put on hold too many times. My kids are growing, my marriage is strong, and my career needs a shot of adrenaline. My goal of finishing at the end of the spring 2018 semester was set intentionally, as it will be when my son graduates from high school. I have a mental image of the picture we will take together in our graduation caps and gowns. It's my motivation!

HOLLY MCDONALD
THE UNIVERSITY OF TEXAS AT EL PASO

Do you provide feedback or feedforward?

PAY IT FORWARD: INSPIRE YOUR STUDENTS TO STRIVE HIGHER

The mediocre teacher tells. The good teacher explains. The superior teacher demonstrates. The great teacher inspires. —WILLIAM ARTHUR WARD

WHAT DOES IT MEAN to be a great teacher? Ward's quote provides a compelling answer to this very question. The great teacher will inspire people to strive higher, reach further, and expand their minds outside the usual and mundane boundaries. I have had three teachers throughout my life who have inspired me to reach for the stars.

> The great teacher will inspire people to strive higher, reach further, and expand their minds.

My first true teacher in life was my father. As hard as he was on me, he saw a potential in me that I did not see in myself until later in life. He had to force me to dig deep inside to achieve all my goals. He once told me that I had some raw talent. However, I needed to dig deep to turn that raw talent into an unbelievable skill set. He always pushed me, without pushing me over the edge, to go further than my own imagination would take me. His work ethic was passed on to me. He inspired me to become an honor roll student, a state baseball champion, and a captain in the US Army. Every one of my major accomplishments has been in honor of my father and the fact that he inspired me to be the best that I could be.

My second teacher was my Taekwondo instructor. She is now an eighth-degree black belt, one of the youngest in the history of the sport. She taught me how to sharpen my mind and my body to be in peak condition. Mental sharpness is always the key to succeeding in life. Wherever the mind goes, the body will follow. That is why mental toughness is so important in life. My master, when she was a young third-degree black belt, tore her ACL and MCL (anterior cruciate and medial collateral ligaments). She was told to quit competing. Instead of giving up, she overcame all the obstacles working against her by grinding her way through physical rehabilitation. Most importantly, she never allowed her mind to stop looking forward. She became one of the best competitors in the sport. When I was paralyzed because of injuries I sustained in my last tour in Afghanistan, I was told that my chances of walking again were 50/50. I used my Taekwondo teacher's lessons and her example of dedication and perseverance to overcome my own struggles. It became my new ethos. Fortunately, I was walking again in two months and my legs were fully functional after eight months. She served as my inspiration to never quit.

Finally, one of the instructors in my major at UT El Paso inspired me to develop a passion for learning and an appreciation for the role that managers play in all daily business activities. Being on the factory floor with the employees is where product quality begins and ends. Inspiring my own employees to do their best work will always serve as the ultimate way to honor this particular teacher. By always striving to learn new things that I can apply in my future job as a manager, I will always strive to improve the lives of everyone around me. Through his inspiration and passion, I will do everything in my power to inspire my eventual employees to deliver their best work. This is what will make me a successful manager.

These three great teachers have inspired me to become a competent individual and a respected member of our society. Their lessons have given me the power to go further than I ever thought I could. Importantly, they were generous enough to give me the power to inspire others to reach for the stars. Pay it forward!

EDWARD GUNDERSON
THE UNIVERSITY OF TEXAS AT EL PASO

What can students learn from each other?

PERSPECTIVES FROM A
NON-TRADITIONAL STUDENT

ALTHOUGH IT HAS BEEN a struggle, I am proud of the progress I have made in my academic career. As a non-traditional, first-generation student, I started at a community college. I worked thirty hours a week throughout my undergraduate years. It took me seven years to accomplish, but I managed to progress from academic probation to earning my associate degree to graduating from UT San Antonio with honors. In order to reach my goals, I examined the most successful students around me and adopted their strategies. It was readily apparent to me that to succeed I needed to emulate their strong study habits, complete my assignments, and attend class. The most important thing, however, was to make school a priority in my life. While it is easy to put work ahead of school or become distracted by technology, students can only benefit from a college education if they actively participate in the process.

This is particularly important for students like me who don't come to college knowing how the game is played. For example, when I started school, I had no idea how much learning I would need to do on my own, and I was not adequately prepared for assuming that role. I also lacked time management skills, relying instead on late-night cramming. Finally, I had to adjust my attitude. Coming out of high school, I was not respectful to my professors and sometimes took advantage of their generosity. I would often plead for extended deadlines, turn in my assignments late, and then hold the professors accountable for my poor grades. In reality, my poor attitude toward school and lack of respect for those assisting me led to early failure. I eventually realized that, in order to succeed, I must take responsibility for my own actions rather than taking advantage of the generosity of others. With this in mind, I was able to change my approach to school and began to succeed as a college student.

Of course, the student is only one-half of the classroom interaction. I believe that, no matter how good or bad a student is, classroom success ultimately hinges on the quality of the teacher. Good teachers genuinely care about the success of their students and show it. They also need to communicate their subject matter in a clear and concise way, to foster discussion in class, and to help students recognize the real-world applications of their work. Finally, good teachers set aside regularly scheduled time to meet with students who need further assistance. These positive actions create a memorable learning experience for students and help them to develop confidence.

In contrast, the actions of a bad teacher can be devastating. When teachers denigrate students, fail to recognize their learning needs, or treat them unfairly, they essentially communicate that they don't value their students enough to share their educational expertise and experience with them.

> Good teachers genuinely care about the success of their students and show it.

When students feel that faculty

don't care about them or don't believe they have the ability to learn, they develop a negative mindset about school, think it is not for them, and may ultimately quit. Fortunately, I was able to find good teachers who helped me to grow and to realize that I could be a successful student, despite my prior experience. Against all odds, I am now a graduate student and hope that I can observe these teachers, as I once observed my fellow students, in order to learn how to be the sort of teacher I have so appreciated in my own life.

CORY KNIGHT

THE UNIVERSITY OF TEXAS AT SAN ANTONIO

Students should not always know what to expect when they come to class.

ENERGIZE THE
LEARNING ATMOSPHERE

I WASN'T ALWAYS a good student. A disastrous first year in college led to a reboot at community college, where I developed some study skills and self-discipline but still managed only a B average. I returned to UT Austin, hoping only for a C average, but surprised myself with straight As semester after semester. What astonished me more, however, was realizing that studying now felt less like a chore and more like an adventure.

What, I wondered, made my courses at UT Austin so exciting? Sorting through my memories of the most engaging lessons and teachers from grade school to the present, I realized that the common denominator was love. In the same way that a smile is infectious, a teacher's love for a topic permeates the content and energizes the learning atmosphere.

> A teacher's love for a topic permeates the content and energizes the learning atmosphere.

In grade school, I recall watching scientist Carl Sagan on television, rapt as he enthusiastically demonstrated concepts such as dimensionality and the properties of light, marveling that "we're all made of star stuff!" In high school, the day that stands out above all others is when our history teacher, Mr. Sagan (no relation), discussed with us in detail his studies of the atrocities of the Holocaust. To this day, I remain deeply moved by his candor and gravity as he taught us what can happen when personal responsibility gives way to "just following orders."

At UT Austin, I've encountered an abundance of professors who have devoted their lives to study and discovery. They radiate this passion in their lectures, in conversations and activities, and by example.

A professor of physical anthropology brought her lectures to life with stories of her work in Madagascar, while a linguistic anthropology professor intrigued us with his novel theories about the origins of language. One philosophy professor shared his love of ancient Greek texts by inviting students to readings at his home, and another held informal salons in which students could engage in any philosophical topic of interest. By curating readings from a vast array of disciplines, an astronomy professor elevated a course on extraterrestrial life to a study of what makes life on earth—and indeed, our own humanity—possible. A physics professor shared his joy for his subject with instructive, entertaining, and often mind-boggling experiments in class.

But the College of Pharmacy raised the bar even higher. Respect for patients and concern for their well-being were not only the underpinnings of every course, but also mirrored universally by staff and faculty in their innovative approaches to education, in their attentiveness to students as individuals, and in their generous support and cultivation of extracurricular learning activities. This had the extraordinary effect of inspiring entire student bodies to adopt the same values. It is a truly special experience to study alongside hundreds of fellow students under a faculty of leading scientists and clinicians who are motivated to excellence by a desire to provide the best possible care to patients and communities.

Gaining some self-discipline and study strategies helped me to pass classes. It was my teachers' love for their fields, their students, and their fellow humans, however, that inspired me to explore, motivated me to challenge myself, and provided me with the finest models for my own development as a clinician, scientist, teacher, and citizen of the world.

JULIETA SCALO
THE UNIVERSITY OF TEXAS AT AUSTIN

What motivates students to come to your class?

CHALLENGE US

ONE OF MY FAVORITE THINGS about UT Permian Basin is that the student body consists of a diverse group of students. I have had classes with students ranging from ages eighteen to fifty-plus. I love the older group of students because they have so much to offer to the class. They also *want* to be there. They are taking time out of their already established lives to be in the classroom with me, who entered college straight out of high school. Sometimes they bring the best perspectives to the lesson. I find that I connect more with them than I do people my own age. In my opinion, they exemplify great students: they want to be there, they are prepared for class, and they do their work. They are excited to be there, and best of all, they know what their time in the classroom is worth.

I write this next sentence with wavering hesitation: *if the only grades taken in the class are those based on discussion boards or open-book tests without a time limit, the students aren't learning.* I like those classes because they are easy, but to be completely honest, I feel they are a waste of my time and money. I have been in many classrooms where anyone with a pulse can get an A. To me, that is not fair. I work hard. I like to be successful. I like to know that my hard work is noticed. However, if a teacher is just there to make a salary and doesn't challenge the students, I do not learn the material. I can get discouraged when *everyone* gets an A but I know I was probably the hardest-working student in the class. In other words, an A is not an accomplishment in those classes.

Professors, please let me show you that I have done my homework, because I work hard on it. Please give me a quiz, because I read the book. Give me some feedback, because I am going to need it later when I start my career. Other students who read this might come at me with pitchforks and torches, but we are at the university to learn and to prepare ourselves for our careers. That is what you are paying for, and if we don't acquire the knowledge now, we are setting ourselves up for failure in the future. We *are* the future. We are the educators, scientists, athletes, and artists who are expected, *very soon*, to teach others, save lives, and inspire.

> Give me some feedback, because I am going to need it later when I start my career.

I want to teach high school English after I graduate. Right now, I am taking classes that teach me how to teach, yet I have learned far more of what to do and what *not* to do from the example of the professors I've had at the university. I have not had any awful professors, but I have had some amazing professors who challenged, taught, and inspired me. These are the teachers from whom I learn what to do. Those teachers make everyone feel heard, and they don't shut students down if they are wrong. These teachers do not show favoritism, or praise specific students for their good work in front of the class, but instead give feedback that will improve every student's work individually. These teachers clearly care for students, and they show this by challenging them and stimulating their minds. These teachers get students excited and engaged with interesting material. These teachers love what they teach. These teachers make students laugh. These teachers can take the most boring subject, such as grammar, and make it one of the most fun and interesting classes in my schedule. These teachers teach.

Students, learn the material to the best of your ability, because you are paying good money for that information. Teachers, challenge us. I want to know that I am successful in the classroom. I want to know that I am learning something. I want to be prepared to inspire.

VICTORIA INMAN-HINESLY

THE UNIVERSITY OF TEXAS PERMIAN BASIN

Do your students think you care
about their learning?

EMPATHY: THE CARE OF AND FOR STUDENTS

EMPATHY IS ESSENTIAL IN TEACHING

EMPATHY—THAT IS, LISTENING to students and caring about what they say—is essential to good teaching. This is not so that teachers can give students what they want. What students want and what they need can be different things. It is because effective teaching is possible only when teachers understand how students experience learning and the learning environment. Empathy for students' experiences is essential for making important decisions about teaching. Notice that in these essays, when students write about qualities that make a great teacher, the focus repeatedly is on a teacher who listens to and is empathic to the student perspective, who understands how a student might feel in a class and how this will affect learning. Empathy for students affects decisions about course objectives, activities, assessments, and overall planning. In order to teach effectively, teachers must understand what students will be thinking and feeling, both regarding the material being learned and the learning process itself. As noted by cognitive psychologist Daniel Willingham in his 2009 book *Why Don't Students Like School?*, "memory is the residue of thought." We will always be better teachers when we remember that what students are thinking and feeling is what they will learn.

Having empathy means that we are tuned in to what students think and feel. The twin components of empathy are perspective-taking and compassion. Some of what students think and feel about the learning process—what it takes to learn, what it means to learn, or even how important it is to learn—may interfere with their learning. The goal is not to make students happy, but to create experiences that will make learning happen by influencing what and how they think, using emotions to motivate them, interest them, get their attention, or direct their behaviors. For example, if I plan an activity for students to answer questions about an assigned reading in small groups, I must consider the students' perspectives: Will the questions prompt higher level thinking or lower level? Will students be emotionally involved in developing thoughtful responses and collaborating with others? Will they be fearful or defensive, preoccupied by feelings of social awkwardness or resentment? Will they understand what is expected and why? Sometimes, it may be helpful to evoke moral outrage in a class, or excitement, or sadness, or confusion. It is essential to know how to use these responses to promote deep and meaningful learning.

Empathy is essential for interacting with students in the classroom. The more teachers understand and therefore can be compassionate about students' experiences and points of view, the more they can help students focus on learning and overcome internal or external obstacles that may arise. For example, I can be a better teacher if I understand that a student who falls asleep in class may be exhausted, rather than unmotivated or lazy (and if they are unmotivated or lazy, I can again ask why). I am a better teacher if I understand that catching the bus on time isn't a learning outcome, and therefore should not determine whether or not a student passes an exam.

Students come with a history of interactions with and subsequent expectations about teaching and learning. Even if some students demand to be taught in a particular (perhaps ineffective) way, they are doing so not because they are "problem" students, but because this is what makes sense from their point of view. It may be that they need a new understanding of how to learn, and understanding that should influence *how* teachers respond. Students are people to be understood, not problems to be dealt with or removed. To teach effectively, we must remember what it feels like to not yet know the things we now know, and help students follow the path toward discovery and understanding.

KAREN HUXTABLE, PHD
UT SYSTEM ACADEMY OF DISTINGUISHED TEACHERS
THE UNIVERSITY OF TEXAS AT DALLAS

THE WALLS THAT DIVIDE
OUR CLASSROOMS

"JUST LEARN WHATEVER YOU WANT because knowledge is unified," ecologist Amory Lovins told me when I interviewed him for my high school newspaper. "All disciplinary boundaries are artificial and don't really exist."

His eyes were uncomfortably magnified through his round glasses as he peered back at me, a kooky grin forming under his bushy mustache.

This guy must be absolutely crazy.

And he was crazy, absolutely bonkers. As our conversation continued, he told me stories of parachuting cats, living on a banana farm, and the adventures of having taxidermied animals throughout his home.

But Amory Lovins was also right. He is a brilliant guy, having saved the US government trillions of dollars in energy costs. Quirky as he is, he knows what he is talking about.

His words clicked with me for the first time months later, during a physics project. The assignment: study the physics and history of a musical instrument, then present your findings and play a song. I chose an unconventional instrument, the wine glass.

First, I studied the glass as science. I spent hours in the

lab, recording volumes and frequencies until I could explain why my glass could sing when its rim was rubbed. I studied it as history, and the glass transformed. I was transported to eighteenth-century England, when dapper gentlemen and lovely ladies paid a fortune to hear its song. I studied it as music, and the glass transformed again. I heard notes, the same ones from my years of playing piano. On the day my project was due, I played "Happy Birthday" on wine glasses for the class.

If I had only studied the glass as physics, it would be nothing more than a generator of sound waves. Instead, I also saw it as a fine art form, an amazing and beautiful instrument. Even then, there was still so much to discover.

Amory Lovins was right: it would have been silly to say that I shouldn't study history or art in physics class. In college, this type of interdisciplinary thinking has become even more critical: What if I could build a statistical model to help me process the data that I had researched in my seminar on hunger? What if I could use my accounting knowledge to better understand the financial hardships of educational reform, which I learned about in my civic engagement class? Soon, everything became connected: Chinese poetry and astronomy, management and philosophy, infinities and biology. The possibilities were limitless.

The more I asked, the more I fell in love with learning. Most recently, I've discovered the intersection between math and poetry. Think of a sonnet: a sestet, an octet, and ten syllables per line: 6, 8, 10? That's a Pythagorean triple. These connections have inspired my Plan II thesis: Poetry sounds beautiful to us musically because it makes sense mathematically.

> The more I asked, the more I fell in love with learning.

Undergraduate education works best when we shatter the walls that divide our classrooms. Students need to be intellectual explorers, searching for the common threads between the disparate course numbers on their schedules. Professors need to be thought partners for students, converting classrooms into laboratories where students can blend educational disciplines.

To me, it seems unthinkable that a business student could spend four years at this university and never step foot into the communication building, or that a biology student might never collaborate with a biomedical engineering major. Each individual field of study at this university is absolutely amazing, but if we think like Amory Lovins and begin to study these fields together, I have a feeling that the whole will be far greater than the sum of its parts.

RACHEL DIEBNER

THE UNIVERSITY OF TEXAS AT AUSTIN

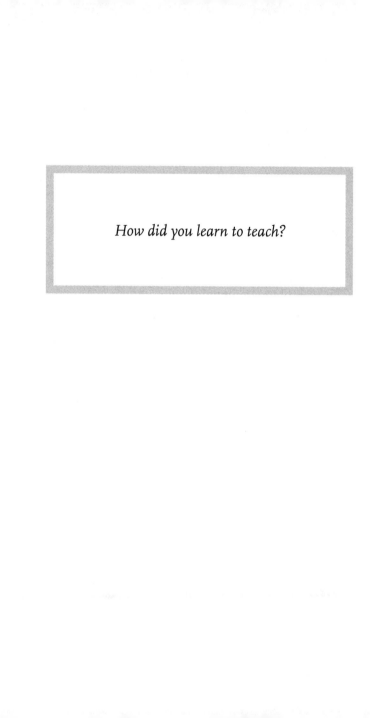

How did you learn to teach?

CARING TEACHERS

IN MY EXPERIENCE, great teachers possess the ability to let their students know that they care about each of them as individuals. This characteristic can be directly linked to their ability to teach well and is a cornerstone of a great teacher. For instance, teachers who make it abundantly clear that questions are encouraged during class indicate their concern that students truly understand the subject. Even during class, if there are just a few students asking the majority of questions on a particular subject, and time is short, such a teacher might say, "We will have to move on to another topic. If you still have questions, see me after class or during office hours, and I will be happy to answer them." By making this statement, the teacher makes it clear that he or she is not ignoring those students and signaling that it will be more productive to have a one-on-one discussion about the topic. When a teacher makes it clear that the student's query is not being disregarded, it helps the student feel safe enough to ask questions. If a teacher moves to another topic without mentioning his or her willingness to meet one-on-one, then those students who still have questions may become self-conscious about asking them. It could even get to the point of hindering the student's capacity to learn.

When a teacher encourages students to meet with him or her outside of class to address questions about the homework or about the concepts discussed in class, it's an indication that the teacher cares. When the teacher says, "I have an open-door policy," and assures us that we are welcome to come and talk about class anytime the door is open, it reinforces the idea that the teacher truly cares about the success of the students. These teachers are often willing to drop whatever they are working on to help their students. Some of my best teachers have non-mandatory, out-of-class reviews for exams, and are willing to accommodate anyone who can't make it to the review. These teachers go above and beyond their basic duties, demonstrating that they care. This approach doesn't just make the students feel comfortable or feel better about themselves, but also helps them master the material. It shows that the teacher cares about the students and is willing to do whatever it takes to make sure they understand the subject. Perhaps I have had teachers who cared about their students but didn't express it enough, so that the students were afraid to ask questions or seek help from the teacher. If they had shown that they cared more often, then their students probably would have done better in their classes.

> If they had shown that they cared more often, then their students probably would have done better in their classes.

RADLEY FEINER
THE UNIVERSITY OF TEXAS AT TYLER

*How is learning an important
part of your teaching?*

WHAT IT TAKES TO BE MEMORABLE

AS A JUNIOR STUDENT in chemistry, I have had my fair share of good and bad courses. Some of them do not mean the world to me; however, there were several amazing classes that made an indelible mark on my life. A memorable class can be either good or bad, but I guarantee that each one of us has had a class to remember. What makes a class good is how the professor teaches and the knowledge gained.

Professors have the power to create a good or bad environment in a class, given that they are in charge the great majority of the time. In order for students to enjoy the class, it is extremely important for the professor to have a positive attitude toward the work. If the professor likes what he or she is doing and is interested in the learning experience of students, the class is going to be more pleasant for both parties. In addition, I like to see that my professors know the subject well. Otherwise, students cannot become interested in the material. Professors have the capacity to transmit their attitude and knowledge to students and make a class memorable.

The knowledge gained is also important for a memorable class. For example, I keep most of my middle school classes in the "sure-I-learned-that-but-I-cannot-remember-what-about-it" part of my brain, whereas I keep a class where we studied the periodic table in my brain's principal warehouse. That is because I learned the periodic table by studying with mnemonics and songs. How much students learn and remember goes hand-in-hand with their overall satisfaction about their performance in the class. If students do their homework and read ahead, they will be more satisfied with their performance. The resulting grade will be based on effort, which impacts significantly the way we remember a class. A memorable class is a balance of performance, how much was learned, and the grade. In fact, when I think of a good class, the first thing that pops into my head is a class where grades are not the main focus.

In conclusion, a memorable class is built on multiple factors, including the professor's attitude and desire to teach, how the material was learned, and how much was learned. It is up to the students to make the most out of a class, but sometimes a professor can make a boring subject more enjoyable than expected. More importantly, as students, we will remember the classes where we made mistakes and had the chance to correct them. That is when knowledge is really acquired. Maybe the information we learned was not related to the course, but each class in its own way leaves us with something to remember.

> A good class is a class where grades are not the main focus.

ALMA CAROLINA ESCOBOSA
THE UNIVERSITY OF TEXAS AT EL PASO

WHAT MAKES A GREAT TEACHER

THERE WILL ALWAYS be someone special in our lives, someone who can open our eyes to see past what is in front of us and help us acquire a deeper understanding of new and pertinent knowledge. This person can provide insight, place concepts in context, and enable us to achieve something that would not otherwise be attainable. Regardless of the exact subject or major, being an active participant in learning and a recipient of someone else's experiences and knowledge is always an act of trust and open communication. Sharing knowledge is what we should hold dear and sacred about teaching. Teaching is all about helping other people succeed in their endeavors. That is exactly what makes a great teacher: the unselfish and kind act of sharing knowledge in a patient and developmental manner.

Patience and perseverance are valuable virtues in teaching. When a teacher attempts to pass on the wisdom gained through hard work, some students for various reasons might resist opening their minds to unfamiliar ideas and new knowledge. It could be because they are not motivated enough, or because they do not know how to

> A great teacher shares knowledge in a patient and developmental manner.

let this knowledge in. These are barriers that teachers confront daily. The teacher needs to determine exactly why this is happening and what needs to be done. Perhaps in some cases nothing can be done. Yet a great teacher is the one who takes the time to figure out what resources might help and makes the effort to persevere, insist, try again, and try again in a different way. It is the great teacher who does not blame the students but keeps trying to get through to them. The great teacher is the one who insists there might be a better way to do things and to help the students learn. The desired goal can be achieved through this kind of determination. This is what fuels an awesome teacher. Recognizing that everyone learns differently is key to extracting the full potential of an individual, and great teachers know how to do that.

Communication is also a vital part of the learning process. In this setting, communication goes beyond words and proper grammar. It includes all the signals that a teacher sends through body language, for example, such as a smile of approval or a frown of disapproval. Great teachers are contagious. An enthusiastic teacher generates curiosity about the subject, and his or her students follow that example every step of the way. Teachers mold their students' personalities with confidence, determination, integrity, and a richer understanding of the meaning of life. It is imperative that society appreciate what they do and replicate their success. Great teachers not only help in advancing the standard of living of their students themselves, but they also advance the well-being of all people associated with their students.

RICARDO RAMIREZ JR.
THE UNIVERSITY OF TEXAS AT EL PASO

Students should not believe everything
you said just because you said it.

THE INTEGRAL ROLE OF
THE PROFESSOR

AN UNDERGRADUATE STUDENT enters college expecting to deepen his or her understanding of a subject and attain the knowledge needed for success in the professional world. However, it soon becomes apparent that fulfilling this aspiration is a long and arduous journey. For guidance on the expedition, students look to their instructors. They hope their instructors will lead them well on this educational journey and help to mold them into the professional people they want to become.

The difference between a model student and an unsatisfactory one is the student's degree of involvement in the class. The most important factor is attending class and lab sessions consistently and actively taking notes during lectures.

> The difference between a model student and an unsatisfactory one is the student's degree of involvement.

Among those students with adequate attendance, the most significant difference between a phenomenal student and an average one is the way in which the student approaches the material. An average student may be able to reproduce the facts and concepts introduced in class upon demand; the extraordinary student, however, works to comprehensively understand the material and integrate it within the framework of his or her current knowledge. By achieving this level of comprehension, a student becomes able to assist his or her struggling peers, able to apply the material meaningfully outside of the course, and able to use the ideas abstractly to arrive at novel conclusions. However, as vital as a student's investment in the class and acquisition of knowledge is to success, the professor carries part of the responsibility, too, because a professor can hinder or facilitate a student's growth and the growth of the model student population.

To promote student success, the professor must communicate expectations and course material clearly and effectively. A good professor must be available to students outside of class for clarification of content. He or she must also be able to recognize the dynamic teaching needs of different students and know how to adapt his or her teaching methods in effective ways for unique student populations. This teaching approach would include expressing new concepts in multiple ways in order to maximize understanding and enable students to integrate the material.

An exceptional professor also keeps the class engaged, using humor and building a connection with students. The use of humor during a lecture serves a dual purpose: it deconstructs the monotony of notetaking, which can otherwise cause students to disengage, and it makes the professor seem more approachable and relatable while still maintaining an appropriate level of formality and professionalism. This quality of relatability distinguishes a merely good professor from a great professor, because it provides a reprieve for struggling students and encourages them to seek supplemental instruction from the professor outside of class. Students feel more comfortable interacting with a relatable professor than with one who is too formal.

A professor who makes the class fun and enjoyable makes it a memorable experience. Memorable, enjoyable classes, although a relative rarity, particularly in the core curriculum, are a joy to attend. An exceptional and passionate professor conveys enthusiasm and interest, qualities that are integral to a remarkable course. Just as an enjoyable experience in the classroom of a passionate teacher is contagious, so, too, is a professor's discontent. Lack of enthusiasm on the part of a professor can be obvious during lectures and can also become diffused among the students.

Thus, the professor is responsible for the development of an enjoyable class experience and for nurturing the academic development of the students. An enjoyable class promotes attendance and participation. Dynamic teaching strategies nourish a meaningful understanding of the course content. The student-teacher relationship itself is dynamic, with the student following the lead of the teacher down the road of comprehension. Without an adroit guide, the student may deviate from the path and lose sight of the purpose of a college education.

JEFFREY MICHAEL KING
THE UNIVERSITY OF TEXAS AT TYLER

What is the best way to end a class?

TEACHABILITY

RETURNING TO COLLEGE as an older adult, I have found that the quality of my professors has made a great impact on me. Maybe it is because I have taught in the intervening space myself, so I realize how much energy good teachers put into their work. In my time, I have been privileged to learn from a few really great college professors. Here are the things I have noticed make professors great.

Great professors make themselves available to their students from day one. Because of the technology available today, this does not have to be in person. It is less about the content of those connections than about making the effort. For a student trying to navigate the sometimes confusing world of higher learning, it helps to know that you can simply ask a question and not be looked down upon. Great professors are available not only outside the classroom, but in the classroom, too, through a willingness to listen and an openness to questions and comments outside of their own agenda.

This leads me to my next point: great professors have teachability. Yes, the professors are the ones teaching, but they should also be

> Great professors
> have teachability.

learning. A bright-eyed student will probably be encountering many of the ideas being presented in the classroom for the first time, while seasoned teachers have been hashing them out for years. However, master teachers maintain an element of teachability that allows students to feel they have something to contribute. If students feel as though they are on a journey with the teacher, then they are more likely to engage.

Great teachers also see themselves as facilitators, rather than just transmitters of information. They can provide information, or access to it, but then they ask students to engage and make it their own. As facilitators, teachers provide students with a place to communicate openly about what they are learning. Great professors allow for—or even push students into—class participation. They provide a platform for students to take the knowledge into their own hands, examine it from different angles, and produce something valuable out of that experience.

That is not to say professors should never disseminate their knowledge. Truly expert professors are knowledgeable masters of their craft. Some classes can offer tons of discussion time among peers, but they leave the students wanting for deeper perspective. Great professors share their knowledge. Doing so is evidence of the fact that they have handled that information for themselves.

Lastly, great professors care about the success of their students. This last item should perhaps be first because, as the old adage goes, "People don't care what you know until they know that you care." I have seen students dismiss professors who seem to be concerned only about their own self-aggrandizement. However, I have also seen caring professors draw students in who would otherwise fall through the cracks. Great professors care about the success of their students because they know the impressions they leave on them are their ultimate legacy.

LENA LIEDTKE

THE UNIVERSITY OF TEXAS AT TYLER

Learning to teach is hard,
and it takes a long time.

TEACHING TO THE MOMENT

IN STEPHEN SONDHEIM'S MUSICAL *Into the Woods*, the Baker's Wife proposes a framework for interpreting the passage of time. The majority of day-to-day life is "plain" and unremarkable, but every person's experience is dotted with "peculiar passing moments," make-or-break interactions that define the structure of an individual's collective memory. Although she recognizes that life cannot be "made of moments," these brief encounters give the ordinary times between them new meaning. As my graduation approaches, I have begun to understand just what the Baker's Wife means: what goes according to plan goes largely unremembered, but what is exceptional remains with us. I don't recall my professors' abilities to post grades on time or stick to the syllabus schedule. What stays imprinted in my mind are the *moments*, those spaces where time and routine briefly cease and sincere human connection takes place, and the instructors who allow them to bloom.

I am fortunate to have had kind and competent instructors across the board. Some professors stood at the front of the class and presented PowerPoint lectures—and while I remember their classes as pleasant experiences, with the passage of time I remember little else. Then there are the instructors who encourage discussion and participation, creating a classroom environment that fosters creativity and the exchange of ideas. In this environment, moments happen, and the instructors who respect their place in the students' learning career prove themselves exceptional. Students articulate how the material affected them. They apply it to their own thoughts and experiences. They synthesize the matter in unexplored ways. They ask questions and critique each other's ideas in a space where all intellects have equal standing. I don't mean to propose that an instructor should spend all of class time discussing subjective feelings. However, allowing a free flow of discussion where students can react freely, experiment, and even be proven wrong accomplishes a big-picture goal, whereas overregulated lesson plans fall short.

Take, for example, the Blackboard discussion board post—a common instructional tool in my classes. Oftentimes, students dutifully accomplish the needs of the prompt and minimum word count, then return to their normal business. However, in a literature class from last semester, one instructor loosened the reins. She allowed students to pick their own topic, as long as it was relevant to the material from recent weeks, and approach it however they felt they could best articulate an argument. Once students began to realize the kind of freedom they had, participation exploded, and moments cropped up across the board. Classmates commented with greater frequency and higher word counts than they were ever required to pro-

> The instructors who respect their place in the students' learning career prove themselves exceptional.

duce. They shared their vulnerable experiences, and others reached out to embrace them. We didn't just learn about literature, but about why it's worth studying—the ways that it simultaneously reflects and influences everything, from the whole society to the heart of the individual. When we felt firsthand the ways that literature changed us as a class, recognizing its power to change society wasn't such a stretch anymore. By the last day before finals, the class was so moved by the way we had bonded that, when we were dismissed, we could not bring ourselves to leave. Instead, we gathered. We talked. We thanked our instructor and each other for the moments that we had experienced emotionally and intellectually. Because our instructor gave us the means to connect to each other, we had been able to see beyond the schedule—and as a result, beyond the grade.

ALLISON PIERCY

THE UNIVERSITY OF TEXAS AT ARLINGTON

Set your learning expectations on high.

ENCOURAGE HONEST DISCUSSION

BACK IN MY SENIOR YEAR of high school, when I wrote essays on why I wanted to go to college, I joked that, besides my anticipation of sophisticated wall décor, after twelve years of primary and secondary education, my conditioned response was to do as I was told.

The real reason was less entertaining and also the exact opposite. College was a means to extricate myself from the inflexibilities ingrained in education, those expectations of students to unquestioningly follow each instruction to the T. I wanted the ability to learn more freely and deeply, and in that sense, I looked forward to better teachers.

But what constitutes a "better" teacher? The differentiating factor, I think, is respect.

An educator respecting students and being respected by them is not equivalent to being well-liked. Years ago, we had a Teacher of the Year Award, voted on by students, and rarely did the best teacher win. Many of my peers instead favored lenient instructors who let students do whatever they wanted, even if those classes were ultimately useless.

> An educator respecting students and being respected by them is not equivalent to being well-liked.

One of the best teachers I've ever had, in contrast, was disliked by my class because of the workload. However, all of us respected her. While taking copious history notes was no one's idea of a good time, we could appreciate her obvious passion for her subject and let her enthusiasm motivate us. She excitedly related events across oceans and centuries, pointed out how they were interconnected, and discussed how they related to our lives, rather than demanding the boring memorization of dates and facts. She did it to encourage us to learn deeply, and we—albeit grudgingly—rose to the challenge.

The idea of learning deeply is especially significant to undergraduate education, in which a greater percentage of students show up because they actually want to venture beyond the surface-level K–12 curriculum. Thus, effective educators must respect students' right to learn, understanding that they are to teach students how to think instead of how to memorize information they could find online. Instead of maintaining an illusion of learning by trying to trip students up on meaningless specifics, such as the color of a literary character's bathrobe, good instructors delve deeply into fundamentals, explaining and contextualizing causes and effects of phenomena while encouraging curiosity by welcoming questions.

Sometimes, respect for students simply boils down to not taking them for complete morons. I've encountered teachers who relied so heavily on other instructors' online materials—such as Khan Academy or Bozeman Science—that students wondered if teaching was really just a matter of walking in and pressing play on a YouTube video. I once had a teacher who was rarely able to answer math homework questions without the help of her answer key. Her lack of preparation translated to not taking us seriously, and we began to feel the same about her.

To facilitate a respectful environment, a skilled professor will bridge the student-teacher divide by encouraging honest, open discussion and giving specific, candid feedback, pointing out how something was nicely done or could have been done better. Distributing praise like Halloween candy to avoid hurting feelings not only dilutes the value of positive feedback but also gives little credit to the students and does them little service. It is just as vital to not patronize as it is to affirm.

I've encountered good and bad teachers during my stint in education, so I recognize the value of considerate instruction. Superficial knowledge is like a coat of paint and spruced-up wall décor. I'm determined to learn something far deeper than that and to retain it long after I receive my degree, and I look forward to the capable professors who will help make that difference.

NICOLE SUN

THE UNIVERSITY OF TEXAS AT AUSTIN

The best students don't always have the best grade in the class.

THE CREATIVE CLASSROOM

SO MUCH TO LEARN,
NO TIME TO THINK!

IN "THE CURIOUS STUDENT," Aarti Bhat observes that "many students come into the college environment never having learned how to think independently. These students are used to cutting corners or relying on someone else's work rather than forming their own independent thoughts—and this is a recipe for disaster in higher education."

In my twenty years of teaching mathematics, I, too, have found that independent creative thinking is becoming more and more stifled, even in higher education. In this modern world driven by money, marketing, and prestige, prepackaged courses purchased from companies are becoming a new norm in our classrooms. I was stunned to see a link to one of these products saying, "Here is your course." Like processed food products that the body does not recognize as food, a prepackaged course shuts down the powers of the mind (of both the instructor and the student) to think and create for itself. Crafty advertisements sporting happy faces make these packages appear attractive, but the very services advertised as helpful are what make them unusable for me.

To illustrate what I mean: One service that companies

provide with the math courses they market is an army of procedures for solving problems. Creative thinking about open questions is replaced by mountains of formulas and methods—procedures that can be replicated and repeated. I have seen students become frustrated with their inability to memorize this mass of methods. And I don't blame them; I wouldn't want to memorize it either. It is much easier to solve a problem by thinking.

Company-made courses also come with handy buttons for checking answers. After you work through a procedure, you can click on a button and see if you got the right answer. But do we really believe that this is a service to our students? On a project for a job, can you click on a button to check your work before submitting it to the boss? If we could only teach our students that after getting an answer, the next step is—again—to think! Does the answer make sense, and how can we test it? Validating your own work builds confidence that will be much more handy in any job than those check-your-answer buttons.

Seeing competition from creativity that flows from the passion and curiosity of the instructor and students, companies that sell courses to higher education are coming up with strategies to mimic creative thinking. But it is forced and artificial, like a fruit-flavored drink that "contains real juice." My students prefer 100 percent fresh pressed juice any day. It leaves us feeling refreshed, exercised, confident, and happy. This is expressed well in the words of a senior math major who told me that in my class, "for the first time, I learned how to think on my own."

BARBARA SHIPMAN, PHD
UT SYSTEM ACADEMY OF DISTINGUISHED TEACHERS
THE UNIVERSITY OF TEXAS AT ARLINGTON

Students should learn to help others to learn.

THE CURIOUS STUDENT

WHAT MAKES A GOOD STUDENT? The most intrinsic quality of good students is a sense of curiosity. After all, why are students here if not to soak up as vast a wealth of knowledge as they possibly can? Another important quality in good students is openness to experience. Quality students know that learning goes far beyond the classroom, and they will take the lessons they learn in lectures with them as they interact with the world (and vice versa). The mark of good students is that they are able to view ideas and theories through different lenses and are willing to listen to a variety of different perspectives, regardless of whether or not they agree with them.

What makes me a good student? I exemplify the two aforementioned traits. I have a thirst for knowledge, often disappearing down rabbit holes of articles for hours to understand ideas better—from the psychology behind Ouija board use or the social construction of a serial killer to how attachment styles affect personal relationships. I love collecting tidbits of knowledge from my different classes and academic pursuits, and I love connecting a theory from one discipline with a concept in an entirely different field of study. As a Plan II and human development major with a Global Business Certificate and minor in sociology, I am the embodiment of a curious, interdisciplinary student. Additionally, I take the time to expose myself to experiences beyond the classroom, from helping welcome students into college life as a Camp Texas counselor to volunteering with underprivileged girls in the Austin area. I contribute to the community around me, and in turn, the people I meet through these avenues also help me to grow. My work in the community greatly complements my academic interests, especially when it comes to my lab research in educational inequality in middle schools throughout Austin. I see firsthand through volunteering what these disparities look like and how they can create significant obstacles for young women. This makes the research that much more real for me.

Now, what constitutes a "bad" student? First of all, I doubt anybody would take very kindly to being labeled a bad student, so perhaps it would be better to think of such students as people facing a tough time or obstacle and thus not succeeding academically. Many students like this have unfortunately been pigeonholed, either by their parents or by prior school systems, and forced into fields of study in which they have little interest. Without passion, how can we expect a student to perform well? Moreover, our current educational system reinforces "busy work" by having students thoughtlessly copying textbooks or Power-Point slides. Many students come into the college environment never having learned how to think independently. These students are used to cutting corners or relying on someone else's work rather than forming their own independent thoughts—and this is a recipe for disaster in higher education.

Much of what constitutes a "good" or "bad" student goes back to how and where they were raised. Did their parents instill a sense of curiosity in them, or bark at them to do chores? Did their teachers encourage critical analysis of topics, or force repetitive, mindless note-taking down their throats? I think that the system in general plays a huge role in a student's mindset and success, and we need to consider this before being so quick to judge students or place them in boxes labeled "good" and "bad." If we want to see more successful students, we need to fix the system that has failed so many of those it has sworn to help.

> If we want to see more successful students, we need to fix the system that has failed so many of those it has sworn to help.

AARTI BHAT

THE UNIVERSITY OF TEXAS AT AUSTIN

Students should see their teachers make mistakes.

CLASSROOMS FULL OF CURIOSITY

A STUDENT'S ACADEMIC DRIVE may initially come from a variety of external factors such as the desire to please parents or earn a good wage. However, as I near my senior year and reflect on my path as an engineering student who desired to pursue a PhD, and then an MD, and who is now firmly set on a JD, I have found that the main motivation behind learning is curiosity. The same curiosity that led us to mix baking soda and vinegar when we were in elementary school to see what would happen does not die out as we mature; it simply matures with us. We may no longer wish to simply observe the fizz and the bubbles of a chemical reaction; instead, we ponder the intricate workings of acetic acid and sodium bicarbonate, seeking a deeper understanding of something that brought us a sense of joy at the age of six. A great student is one who strives to keep the curiosity alive amid the stress of a college curriculum. They are the students who are determined not simply to do well in the class, but to continue building a matrix of knowledge about interesting topics. Perhaps more importantly, it is naive to assume that curiosity belongs only to the accomplished student. Curiosity is present in all of us, giving all of us the opportunity to be great.

Curiosity is not the exclusive domain of the student, either, as great teachers remain curious about what they teach and about whom they teach. Curious teachers open doors for students—not only by answering homework questions, but also by finding opportunities to delve deeper into the content and draw students in. Curious teachers are approachable and interested in navigating individual student-teacher relationships regardless of the perceived

> Great teachers remain curious about what they teach and about whom they teach.

academic level of any given student. This is the teacher who may be teaching the introductory humanities class to a group of engineers, but whose passion for the material taps into the curiosity that exists within even the most initially disinterested student.

The greatest teachers are not always the ones who are most recognized as such; nor are the greatest students always the ones holding the highest GPAs. The greatest students are the ones who can identify what keeps them genuinely curious, who take the time to find the story within the topic, and who work toward a greater understanding for their ultimate success. Likewise, the greatest teachers tap into that curiosity and nourish the students' understanding.

DELIA APPIAH MENSAH
THE UNIVERSITY OF TEXAS AT DALLAS

A great professor asks for
and listens to feedback.

TRUE EDUCATION

WE WERE NOT in a classroom, and there was no teacher present—but a Viking! The bottom of his helmet was chipped and appeared too big for his head. Nonetheless, he stood proudly upon his ladder, sword in hand, and another gleaming blade stuck out of a Styrofoam block, which doubled as a coffee table. Oscillating before him like a punching bag was a monstrous claw, the significance of which went over our heads.

Painted on the ceiling and spilling down the walls were words of wisdom from William Blake, W. B. Yeats, and others. Each sentence was engulfed in flames,

> "The Unfolding of the Imagination Is the Only True Education."

seemingly trapping my peers and me in the room. Blossoming in their midst, student artwork beckoned us to join in an unknown battle. Looming above our heads was another inscription: "The Unfolding of the Imagination Is the Only True Education." Our innocent minds prevented us from fully comprehending the meaning of that quote, but as long as we were in his "learning haven," the Viking would make sure we lived by it.

He coaxed us into his classroom by reading fairy tales.

Each title brought up happy memories of being tucked into bed, hearing a parent's soothing voice tell of a happily ever after. But there would be no happy endings here, either for our ignorance or our childhood.

"*This* is the beginning of the end," the Viking would say.

College was looming over our heads like a shaggy claw, and after that, what would we do with our lives? Would we be artists? Or work inside a gray cube?

"Nay! Rage. Rage against the dying of the light!" the Viking yelled, pointing his sword at the Dylan Thomas quote.

When students tilted their heads like puppies, full of questions, most teachers would explain themselves, and they customarily provided a simple plan for students to follow. But the Viking walked a fine line between insanity and genius. He had a syllabus for us, but getting through his class was like traveling through a bamboo forest. We could see how much farther we had to go, but there was no straightforward path toward that final destination.

In order to get to the spot where the Viking stood in a clearing, we had to answer a series of questions within our journals. Therefore, our responses and chosen routes tended to differ. Once we were reunited with the Viking, he would tell us what we should have learned from our travels.

Not every student made it through the bamboo forest. No matter how many easy routes some of the students attempted, the bamboo would snap back and deny them passage. Accepting that they wouldn't reach the clearing, they quietly waited for the fires in the forest to subside, so they could leave the learning haven for the normal world. These students preferred gazing upon white walls, white boards, and empty sheets of paper. They were hungry for a worthy SAT essay, and a class adorned with the label "AP" appeared challenging. But for those of us who wanted to wander through a complex world of art, we knew where the real challenge lay.

With our final tests handed in, the Viking laid them upon the Styrofoam block, picked up his blade, and stabbed them. The test was more than a grade; it was a gauge to see what experiences we had gained since losing our innocence on day one. We either slew our ignorance with the Viking's wisdom, or we let adversity defeat us. Unlike those who gave up wandering, my peers and I chose to follow those before us, who walked among the flames, and graduate from the Viking's learning haven with a fire raging.

LEA ARISTA
THE UNIVERSITY OF TEXAS AT ARLINGTON

*How does a teacher know
when a class has gone well?*

LEARNING HOW TO LEARN

THERE IS SO MUCH INFORMATION one can learn in school. Trigonometry, calculus, and the principles of physics and thermodynamics have found a comfortable home in my brain over the past few years. I was a twenty-six-year-old junior majoring in mechanical engineering when I realized that I had yet to acquire the most important skill that an education can provide. That is, I had yet to learn how to learn.

Allow me to explain. While studying math, physics, and engineering, I had relied almost completely on my ability to memorize to pass and do well on quizzes and exams. Do well on exams and you get a good grade in class, right? Then it hit me one day. Was I leaving my classes with anything more than good letter grades? Or was I just checking them off a list of classes I had to complete in order to receive a degree? As I had finished each class, had my mind internalized the subject, so that I could use my knowledge to help solve the world's problems? The thought hit me almost as hard as the final I took in Linear Algebra just a few months ago. That class, that instructor, and that horrible final helped me realize that I was going about my learning in the wrong way.

All semester, my Linear Algebra professor had stressed the importance of understanding as opposed to just getting answers. She had emphasized that punching numbers into a calculator and then jotting down an answer was not doing math. Who cares if you can solve a 7×7 matrix system?

> Understanding how to learn is a necessary skill to succeed in the classroom as well as in life.

"Explain to me why the calculations you are doing really give a solution to that specific problem," she would say, "and then you might be worth something."

Those weren't her exact words, but that's how I perceived her point. Understanding the path to a solution and having the ability to explain why the answer is correct—or not—is far more important than merely coming up with the correct result through memorized algorithms. Come finals day, my old habits of memorizing steps to certain problems and praying that similar problems would be on the final sealed my fate. The test was composed solely of problems asking "how" and "why," not the "what" and "which" like I had hoped. It was a day of reckoning. You could call it my most embarrassing moment as a college student: I turned in a final exam that was only about 20 percent complete. I felt like I had learned nothing, due to my lack of meaningful learning and studying. As horrible as that experience was, it has been, by far, the most beneficial exam I have taken in my college career.

Since that test, I have pledged to study differently. I have made a commitment to learning in a more purposeful way. I am now dedicated to understanding the ideas and reasons behind the techniques, so that I can apply them and modify them for any situation. Understanding how to learn is a necessary skill to succeed in the classroom as well as in life. Memorization is not learning. Learning is understanding, understanding is comprehension, and comprehension is knowledge.

ALEXANDER TRENT CHRISTENSEN
THE UNIVERSITY OF TEXAS AT ARLINGTON

What do teachers learn from their students?

THE SIGNATURE OF
A GREAT PROFESSOR

GOOD TEACHERS PRESENT content and challenge students. Great teachers stand out, because they accomplish these goals in a different way. Much like the curator of an exhibit in a gallery or museum, professors may—or may not—choose, arrange, and display course content in a way that heightens its uniqueness and significance, inviting students to accompany them on a journey of discovery. Although the subject matter may fascinate a teacher, often the delights of discovery remain unexplored by students because of the course design and presentation. Great teachers are not only fascinated by the material but are also able to design and present it in a way that draws students in.

The learning platform provides the first glimpse of the course with the customary syllabus, calendar, list of readings, and perhaps illustrations and photos. Good professors accomplish all of this in an organized way. Great professors, however, go beyond these basic requirements, not only showcasing what is to be learned in the course, but also hooking students' interest. Including well-organized, easy-to-access modules with extraordinary visuals, such as photos and portraits of key figures related to the subject under study, with varied colors, textures, settings, and landscapes, all add variety and pique curiosity. This technique not only shows attention to detail, but models the professor's creativity and ability to present a unique synthesis of the material. Great teachers design content that stands out, rather than a clone of other professors' work. Great professors show students not only their expertise in their discipline, but also their personality and enthusiasm about what they do and how they do it. When great professors stamp their courses with their signature, showing individuality and creativity, students will remember what they learned long after the semester ends.

Great teachers recognize that online and hybrid courses can be just as exciting as face-to-face classes and try to connect with distance learners. In online courses, the only way students may ever "see" the instructor is through video recordings and video conferencing. But just as the professor is real to students in face-to-face courses, students need to see the professor in distance education. At the beginning of the semester, professors can make videos to introduce themselves and the course as a way for the student to connect with the professor. Videos of the professor's lectures, even if brief, replicate the "realness" of the teacher in face-to-face courses. Creative alternatives to computer-based testing and written tests include administering oral exams by video conferencing. These strategies go beyond posting links to videos made by someone other than the instructor. Because online students sometimes feel disconnected from their professors, seeing their faces and hearing them talk encourages student engagement.

Great professors embrace the philosophy that first they teach people, and secondarily they teach subject matter. Face-to-face, or by phone or video conference, they check in with students regularly. Asking how the course is going encourages students to ask questions and engage in discussion about challenging assignments. Asking about student responses to readings, arguments, and assignments encourages critical thinking, allowing for validation of student perceptions or an opportunity for the instructor to

> Great professors embrace the philosophy that first they teach people, and secondarily they teach subject matter.

make suggestions about alternate perspectives. Being a great professor takes time and effort; it requires the professor to go beyond finding the most convenient way to teach. Students appreciate this. In a course taught by a great professor, students discover that something of ultimate importance has happened: transformative teaching results in transformative learning.

What more could I ask for?

MARY ROSE PIHLAK

THE UNIVERSITY OF TEXAS AT TYLER

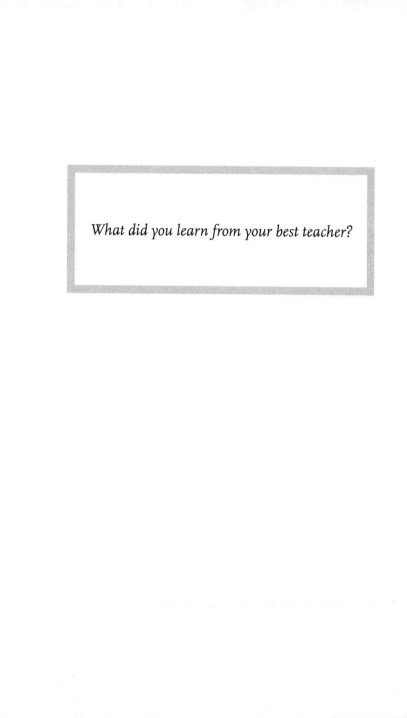

What did you learn from your best teacher?

THINK INSIDE THE BOX

ONE OF THE GOALS of great educators, inarguably, is to teach students to think outside the box—meaning to examine methods of solving problems outside the commonly accepted processes. One mark of good students is the ability to implement this approach throughout their education and their career. However, I would argue that the mark of a great student is to also think *inside* the box.

As the daughter of a Marine, I was educated in schools domestic and abroad, and one thing this experience taught me was that most educators teach about the box. For example, let's examine a right triangle. Most people, given the values of a and

> The mark of a great student is to also think *inside* the box.

b, the sides adjacent to the right angle, can determine the value of c, the hypotenuse, based on the Pythagorean Theorem they learned in grade school: $a^2 + b^2 = c^2$. This is the box.

Thinking outside the box would be to find c using ideas other than the Pythagorean Theorem, such as the trigonometric functions tangent and secant. Finding a solution quickly is not the goal when thinking outside of the box.

Now we come to thinking inside the box. Here we need

to ask ourselves questions. We need to dig through what makes the box, much like scooping out the pumpkin pulp and examining the seeds. Why does $a^2 + b^2 = c^2$? Who first suspected that this was true? What problem originally needed to be solved?

This is a mathematical example, and as a math major, these questions are natural for me to ask. In other classes, such as history, I am less inclined to ask who, how, what, and why. But I should!

By asking these probing questions and digging into the box, students become more and more inquisitive and learn what the box really is and how it came to be. This brings them opportunities for contributing to the conversation as an informed participant. Looking into the box to understand a concept deeply and from various angles allows students to create cross-disciplinary relationships. For example, knowing that drone bees come from unfertilized eggs, a phenomenon in biology, may lead to the conclusion that a single bee's family tree expands on a Fibonacci sequence, a mathematical concept.

So in addition to thinking about and outside of the box, challenge yourself to think inside the box.

ERICA DAVIS

THE UNIVERSITY OF TEXAS AT ARLINGTON

What did you learn from your worst teacher?

LIFE LESSONS

OUR REACH AS INSTRUCTORS IS
FURTHER THAN WE WILL EVER KNOW

IN THE FALL OF 2018, I volunteered to teach a new honors undergraduate course, Sports and Crime, which blended one of my main personal life interests, sports, with my main academic interest, crime, and my new research program linking the two together. Along with several journal articles and case studies (such as the Penn State University scandal involving Jerry Sandusky and Joe Paterno), I selected two books for the class, *Cheated: The UNC Scandal, the Education of Athletes, and the Future of Big-Time College Sports* and *Violated: Exposing Rape at Baylor University amid College Football's Sexual Assault Crisis.* Each week, my twenty students and I read, reflected, and discussed very controversial issues at the intersections of sports, antisocial and criminal behavior, and institutions of higher learning.

These were difficult readings, involving child sexual abuse, real grades for fake classes, rape, drug use, lies, and cover-ups. For many students, some of these topics hit close to home, but for others it was a rude awakening to learn about what has gone on at some universities—at least the universities that get caught. The discussions were lively and challenging, with students sometimes disagreeing with each other—and doing so quite forcefully, but backed with research and not just opinion. All the while they struggled to balance the rights of the accused with the atrocities that they were purported to commit. And then they grappled with how to make more effective policies going forward.

One of the many highlights of teaching this course was that students would report back to the class about discussing the readings with their friends and parents—some of whom had graduated from the universities in question. For them, the readings turned from pages in a book into reality on the phone or over a meal.

Seeing how a simple fifty-minute lecture in a classroom could go beyond space and time and touch countless others was one of the classroom highlights of my over twenty-five-year teaching career. That is the power of teaching in a classroom in real time, when we look into each other's eyes and open up our ears and minds to engage, challenge, and be challenged, and then take that interaction and spread it throughout the world. The connections made in the classroom are not just between the students and the instructor, but reach out in many ways. We may hear about some of them but never realize the full extent of these connections. Henry Adams was right, after all, when he wrote, in *The Education of Henry Adams*, that "a teacher affects eternity; he can never tell where his influence stops." Teaching and mentoring are the gifts that keep on giving, and such connections are the biggest privilege we have as faculty.

ALEX R. PIQUERO, PHD
UT SYSTEM ACADEMY OF DISTINGUISHED TEACHERS
THE UNIVERSITY OF TEXAS AT DALLAS

CROSSING PATHS
AND TYING THREADS

I AM WRITING this at a long picnic table on the newly re-designed Gregory Plaza and Speedway Mall in the center of the UT Austin campus. Under the cool shade of towering oak trees, my feet comforted by the close-grained brickwork beneath my shoes, I can close my eyes and almost feel I am on an Italian piazza. The gentle cadences of voices discussing Plato or linear algebra or the pasta salad for dinner last night; the soft shuffle of students, faculty, and staff strolling across campus; the hum of bicycles, the faint *beeps* of construction machines, and the animated conversation of club recruitment volunteers at the tables lining the Mall: these all make for a stimulating and peaceful midday scene, a minutely choreographed yet wholly improvised representation of university life.

Universities thrive on diversity and the cross-pollination of ideas that feed thought and discovery. The best buildings and outdoor spaces on university campuses—such as the one I'm sitting in—encourage such activity. The best university students successfully navigate the array of ideas and resources, synthesizing what they learn and igniting new threads of discourse. As a Plan II Honors student, I have developed an appreciation for the value of a truly interdisciplinary education. The challenges of taking courses in philosophy, modern physics, creative writing, urban studies, and other subjects in conjunction with each other have strengthened my ability to think beyond the individual disciplines and observe how each resonates with the other.

There is something deeper happening, however, than exposure to many disciplines, a quality that makes someone a great student no matter the program or field of study: a love of learning (*philomathy*, from the Greek). A love of learning pushes students to find something of interest in any lecture, discussion, text, or assignment they may be faced with, however mundane it may seem, and find wisdom in it. It makes them keener observers, broadening their consciousness as they seek to learn from the ordinary details of life. And it elevates their work, enabling them to craft syntheses of new ideas that tie together seemingly disparate strands.

Similarly, the key quality in great teachers is not mere mastery of a discipline but a commitment to the value of learning. The best teachers have a love of learning themselves and recognize that there are important things any student can learn from the material they teach. They have a passion for their discipline and work daily to show their students that it is something worth being passionate about. They read and learn widely, with the understanding that broad knowledge will help them develop new insights and create curricula that resonate with and inspire students in more than one way.

The most memorable class experiences galvanize both students and teacher. They begin with a call to action—the teacher explains why they are teaching the class, why the student is taking it, and what the student can and should hope to learn. The teacher lectures clearly, concisely, and energetically. Whatever the format of the class, there are opportunities for the students and teacher to exchange ideas. The assignments challenge the student to apply the concepts they have learned to other disciplines or their life experiences. The teacher sees the class as a learning experience for themselves as well as a simple imparting of knowledge. Ideally, both student and teacher depart with a desire to pursue further ideas in the discipline. Above all, the best classes don't take themselves for granted.

At one point while I was sitting here, writing this piece, a student approached me and inquired whether she could interview me briefly for a journalism class. I enthusiastically accepted, and she asked me about social media and its relationship to political engagement. Though I didn't cite Rousseau or explain the theory of mirror neurons, my responses drew on things I'd learned from philosophy and neuroscience, literature and social theory—and the whole interaction was a striking example of the way urban design can provoke connections and build community. Like great public spaces and universities, great students, teachers, and classes are crucibles of thought, experience, and love. In the end, life's too short not to be passionate about all you can do to further the pursuit of knowledge and exploration.

> Above all, the best classes don't take themselves for granted.

GABE COLOMBO
THE UNIVERSITY OF TEXAS AT AUSTIN

The best students are
the ones who _____.

THE OPPORTUNITY TO
CHANGE THE FUTURE

THE FUTURE RESTS in the hands of those who educate the young adults of today. Educators shape the future on a daily basis. Each interaction with a great teacher, no matter how small, might have a profound impact on a student's life. Yet there are teachers who, failing to recognize the opportunity to change the future, settle for merely adequate teaching. This situation seems even worse when you consider that countless students seek out these mediocre teachers because it is the easy thing to do. The truth is that all students need a professor who demands excellence and who challenges them to produce their best work because he or she believes in them. Although most students do not seek out these demanding teachers, these are the ones who can truly shape the future of their students by choosing to deeply invest in them.

> The truth is that all students need a professor who demands excellence and believes in them.

While many students seek an easy A, challenging classes truly impact their lives. A student will typically invest more time in a challenging class than in an easy one and will learn more from it. Most students can pass easy classes without learning anything that will have a significant impact on them. A challenging class not only teaches us to think differently, but also frequently involves the application of concepts to real-life situations. This application ends up aiding the students in the long run, no matter where they go in life, no matter what the circumstances. Good teachers always demand excellence because they know mediocrity will not help their students in the future.

Because great teachers don't settle for a normal, easy class, they make their students their first priority. One of the greatest teachers I ever had was a mother of five who had returned to school to teach. She was tough. She would not let us get away with anything; she knew every excuse, every reason we could come up with to do less than was expected. However, she also made us her first priority. She made herself available so that struggling students could come to her office whenever they needed her. She answered emails almost instantly, no matter the hour of the day or night. She treated us not just as students but also as people whose future lives depended on her actions. She loved teaching, and everyone knew it. This caused many of us to love her classes even when we struggled. We knew that, no matter what, we were her priority. She did not find joy in making us work hard; she challenged us because she wanted us to excel. She showed us that great teachers will make their students their first priority because great teachers are future-oriented.

What made her a great teacher was the fact that she believed in us. The realization that we were her first priority compelled most of us to try to do our best. She lit a fire even in the most timid of students. She cared about us and invested so much time in us that we felt we had an obligation to respond in kind. Having a teacher believe in you empowers you to push forward, even when it is very hard. Great teachers believe in their students because they know the future rests on their shoulders.

HOPE NELSON
THE UNIVERSITY OF TEXAS AT EL PASO

How much do grades matter to you?

STUDENTS OF THE WORLD

MOST OF US would like to consider ourselves decent, hardworking students as we travel through our college career. We should know how to manage our time wisely for each course we take, have our weekly planners ready with the correct due dates written in, and access the proper tools to score that perfect A. Yet, as graduation day draws near, I have come to realize that to be a truly excellent student, other, less measurable factors must come into play.

One thing I've learned is that we students are all on this journey together, especially once we're in classes for our major. I cannot overemphasize the importance of trying to develop good relationships with at least one or two people in each course you take. You will see many familiar faces as you complete your major. It is always a good idea to have someone else to collaborate and study with, especially if you need help understanding a text from a different perspective and seeing it in a different light. I learned that this approach is very helpful when you are writing a long paper because a fellow student may spot writing errors you missed, help you reword that sentence you spent far too much time editing, or have other useful input. Two heads are always better than one, even more so if both people are dedicated to the assignment.

> Breaking out of our comfort zones in the classroom is one of the most important actions we can take.

Breaking out of our comfort zones in the classroom is, by far, one of the most important actions we can take to truly grow as a person and as a student. Interacting with one another, especially in the classroom, is crucial for our own development, because it fosters open-mindedness about ideas that are different from our own. Truly listening to and considering each other's interpretations, actually talking with one another in a civil discussion, allows students to form new connections with each other.

I really needed to break out of my shy shell this past semester during a literature course I was enrolled in because group discussions were held every class meeting. We were required to break into small groups and discuss how we each interpreted the assigned readings. Each group member was assigned a different role: moderator, recorder, time keeper, and the one many students feared, reporter, the one who had to present the group's ideas to the whole class. Although a seasoned student, I am generally a shy person, so being the reporter and putting myself out there was a big deal for me; speaking out in front of a large class wasn't easy. However, as soon as I embraced the fact that literature is open to many different interpretations, I learned to relax. These group discussions boosted my self-esteem, and I can now express my thoughts more clearly, staying cool and collected when I speak in front of an audience.

I can say with confidence that this journey has taught

me how to remain open-minded in any given situation, which makes it easier to relate to people and connect with them wherever I am. I've learned that we must always be students of our beautifully diverse world, and not just in the classroom. We need to stay intellectually curious and learn from one another by being humble, staying civil, and being considerate of each other's ideas, especially when they are different from our own. Each time we form a new connection, whether inside or outside of the classroom, we take one more step toward becoming students of the world, a remarkable achievement.

JESSICA HAUGHT
THE UNIVERSITY OF TEXAS RIO GRANDE VALLEY

Are you smiling when class is over?

HERALD OF DISCOVERY

THE STUDENT, like all matter, finds himself or herself most comfortably in a state of rest. A student may hear without listening and in the lecture hall may be surrounded by ideas but challenge none of them. It is therefore the primary objective of the teacher to coax the student from this lackadaisical attitude and stimulate critical thinking. In order for a student to engage in the learning process, the teacher may structure the classroom in a way that challenges the student to test his or her own preconceptions. Only by formulating a hypothesis and testing a result can a student fully understand the implications of the material.

When a professor, before delving into a subject, asks students to write down everything they possibly can about the topic at hand, the students are forced to come to terms with the limits of their understanding. Here, at the fringes of comprehension, curiosity thrives. By requesting hypotheses from their students, a history professor, for example, can illustrate the unfathomable difficulty of a political decision, or a math professor can demonstrate the ingenuity of a proof. If that extra step of forming a hypothesis is not taken, the history student might leave the lecture as a harsh arbiter of historical judgment, or the math student might see the proof as inevitable. Without a hypothesis, students lose their engagement with the material and their appreciation for the discovery of knowledge.

We live in an age of instant gratification. If I want to know the answer to nearly any question in any field, all I have to do is search the Internet for an expert's opinion. Some critics argue that the Internet hinders our ability to recall knowledge. However, the tool can be equally empowering. With the near totality of human knowledge at our fingertips, education can now focus on fostering intelligence rather than knowledge. A student need not be told ideas, but rather needs to learn how to navigate a world flooded with ideas.

In order to train a student to effectively sort through ideas for truth, a professor can postulate a counter-hypothesis. Clever instructors anticipate the preconceptions of their students and can plan this counter-hypothesis accordingly. In this way, they can approach the most polarizing topics with the aim of exploring multiple perspectives. If two arguments have slightly different premises, even sound logic can lead them into radically opposing viewpoints. By challenging the students' hypotheses, professors can force them to confront the nuances of critical thinking and prepare them for a lifetime of decision-making.

Education at its core should prepare individuals for the society in which they will participate. To be a world citizen, one must be able to think for oneself and challenge the origins of one's own beliefs. Those who can engage in

> Education at its core should prepare individuals for the society in which they will participate.

critical thinking will instinctively generate and test hypotheses about their daily lives. Teachers consequently merit the claim that their profession is the noblest, for they teach their students the art of discovery.

GEORGE WALTERS
THE UNIVERSITY OF TEXAS AT AUSTIN

What could you do better in the next class?

REPEAT AFTER ME

I SWALLOW AS I SKIM the lines of Korean characters, printed in a seemingly endless pattern of 이에요s and 저는s and 한국s. Zeke lets out a low whistle. Kristi inhales sharply. My eyes meet Dajin's across the room; we exchange a look of disbelief. I think this is the most intimidating sight I have seen in my three weeks of Korean 1.

But Kim Seonsaengnim appears unaware of our shock. She stares at the textbook page replicated on the screen with her mouth firmly set in that indifferent expression that makes her seem undaunted by any task. It's amazing; I could have mistaken her for an undergraduate student like me if it weren't for the fact that she is always so *confident.*

It's almost as if she thinks we're going to be alive after this exercise.

"시작!" she says. "Repeat after me. 마이클-씨 는 한국 사람 이에요."

We follow along in stuttering, bumbling Korean, our tongues tripping over the ㅋs and our lips contorting into 요s. It is painful listening to ourselves attempt to pronounce this passage; I can only imagine how Kim Seonsaengnim feels. When we finish, we look up at her in unease.

But without batting an eye, she says, "Good."

My classmates and I exchange sheepish looks—we know we were anything but *good*.

Kim Seonsaengnim smiles, acknowledging our embarrassment but unflinchingly continuing forward. "Do you all know what this means?" she asks.

A hand shoots up in the air: Tatiana, the girl with the bright purple hair who helped me master the Korean alphabet, tells us, "It means *Michael is Korean.*"

"Correct. Now everyone say, '저는 미국 사람.'"

After we have done so, she asks, "This means what?"

Ling flips through her textbook. "It means . . . *I am American.*"

"Good. 미국 means America."

"미국," I hear Zeke whisper to himself.

"What other countries are you all from?" Kim Seonsaengnim asks.

Immediately, my classmates begin calling out names of countries.

"How do you say *Jamaica*?" Jamelia says.

"자메이카," Kim Seonsaengnim tells her, and then turns to the class. "Everyone say 자-메-이-카!"

"자-메-이-카," we chant.

"How about *China*?" Janice questions.

"중국. Everyone say 중국."

"중국!"

Kim Seonsaengnim teaches us how to say Italy, Vietnam, India, Mexico. My eyes sweep the classroom; I had never realized how *diverse* we are. The rigor and difficulty of these past three weeks have brought us all together—I

> The rigor and difficulty of these past three weeks have brought us all together.

feel like I've known everyone here *forever*—but it had never dawned on me how many different places we are from. I am an Indian girl in America learning how to speak Korean with classmates from all across the world. I am bonding over a language different from mine with people I would usually never have the opportunity to talk to. Everyone is repeating the names of their countries, telling their seatmates that they are Korean, they are Mexican, they are Filipino.

And standing in the middle of all this is Kim Seonsaengnim, smiling at us with that steadfast confidence. She watches as we read through page 43, Conversation 1 again, replacing *Michael* with our own names and repeating the words on the page until our pronunciation is somewhat acceptable. It's funny how something as small as learning how to say our countries' names in Korean has reinvigorated us, made us face these daunting passages with enthusiasm. It has made it more *personal* to us.

By relating an unfamiliar language to concepts we are familiar with, Kim Seonsaengnim has increased my love for Korean.

Page 43, Conversation 1.

Looks like I'm still alive after all.

SURABI RAO
THE UNIVERSITY OF TEXAS AT AUSTIN

What's one big idea students should
remember after each class?

CONNECT THEIR FUTURE
TO THE CLASS

EVERY STUDENT WANDERS into a classroom thinking, "Why does this class matter?" If they said it out loud, any teacher would be wounded. The entire lecture for the day could be completely derailed.

However, it is a vital question that needs to be answered, because students rely on what they learn to survive in the real world. Whether it is history, literature, science, math, or even art, there is always at least a subconscious goal to seek out knowledge that will become beneficial to you or others in the future. It is important for the teacher to remember this instinct when lecturing in the classroom, because emotion and survival are powerful tools in the creation of memories. Applying this ideology in the classroom will also gain the teacher respect, because the students will recognize that the teacher values them and their lives and future. Ultimately, if a teacher helps students learn the skills necessary to prosper in life, then that teacher has completed his or her duty.

It is well understood that algebra, basic math, reading, writing, logic, and critical thinking are common and useful skills to have in the world; what students often disparage are the deeper subjects that involve higher skills to accomplish, such as physics, calculus, or biochemistry. In these classes, it's especially important to relate the material to everyday life. For example, if a professor is teaching about integrals in calculus, he or she could mention the fact that technicians use integrals in developing new hardware for computers, that astrophysicists need integrals when calculating luminosity or the sizes of stars, or that financial advisers use them for cost/profit analyses. The same professor could elaborate further, noting that biologists use them when analyzing population size and patterns, economists use them when looking at supply and demand, and chemists use them for determining the electron probabilities of atoms or molecules. There are still other fields that use integrals for quick calculations in complex situations.

Many students must take these upper-level classes to finish their core requirements but do not wish to specialize in these fields, and if they do not understand the usefulness of the essential concepts or formulas they are learning in the class, they may soon forget them. By mentioning various fields of interest and tying them to a concept or principle, a professor can bring relevance to the material they are trying to convey. The students will realize that the subject matter is not something to be relegated to geniuses in their highly specialized experiments or theorizing; rather, common folk use these fundamental concepts in everyday life. When students know that what they are learning can be used in their everyday lives, their minds will be opened to the endless possibilities of what they can achieve, limited only by imagination itself.

Short-term and long-term memory both come into play. Short-term memories form in the prefrontal cortex, whereas long-term memories form in the hippocampus. Emotionally driven episodes, including survival scenarios, have a much greater prospect of being stored in long-term memory. Life is survival: we exist today because our ancestors survived. Our instincts are heavily ingrained within us, and there is no

> When students know that what they are learning can be used in their everyday lives, what they can achieve is limited only by imagination itself.

escaping the laws of nature. Education in any form should take real-life applications into account in any lesson being taught, for our minds' most important responsibility is to ensure the safety of the individual and his or her respective members. By understanding the mind and how it works, a professor can therefore improve students' memory and cognition.

TREV FRANKLIN THOMPSON
THE UNIVERSITY OF TEXAS AT TYLER

Whose job is it to inspire students?

OUR CAMPUS PRESIDENTS

FACULTY AND TEACHING EXCELLENCE

YEARS AGO, John Steinbeck wrote, "I have come to believe that a great teacher is a great artist and that there are as few as there are any other great artists. Teaching might even be the greatest of the arts since the medium is the human mind and spirit."

At UT Arlington we are privileged to have some of the greatest artists in the land—through their teaching they touch lives and inspire their students and the rest of us. They help each student create a masterpiece from a dream and from hopes, and in doing so they transform the present into a brilliant future. They also exemplify what it means to be a true *research university*, one that is dedicated to discovering new knowledge and ensuring that the first to have the advantage of it, and those immersed in the process of discovery and inquiry, are our own students. Too often, we forget this simple context. A truly great university is distinguished not just by the scholarly titles and achievements of the faculty, but also by the integration of the work of the faculty through their teaching, and by the commitment of students to ensuring a better future for themselves, their families, and the communities in which they reside and work.

Many universities try to gain a reputation for excellence

by constraining the number and quality of incoming students to the very highest-achieving students, using a range of metrics to define what can at best be considered arbitrary determinants of prior performance as related to ensuring future success. Faculty at UT Arlington have proved time and again that, while the quality of the input stream is important, it is what we enable and encourage while the students are here that largely determines the quality of the output. This is what public universities, especially the top research institutions, have always been about—access to excellence that enables transformation of the world: this is Abraham Lincoln's living legacy—the triumph of human potential, of merit over class and status.

Teaching excellence goes far beyond the formal delivery of lectures and interactions within the four walls of a classroom or laboratory. It encompasses the delivery of knowledge, the igniting of a spark that changes a student's life, the mentorship that nurtures

> It is what we enable and encourage while the students are here that largely determines the quality of the output.

a student's curiosity and intellectual passion, and the sage guidance that helps the student through rough patches—in academics and life. These are true teacher-scholars, the core of UT Arlington, serving as a link between the latest discoveries and the transference of those discoveries to knowledge and success for thousands of students. Our students represent the promise of the future, the vision of achievements and success, the ability to dream lofty dreams, and the possibility of changing lives through education.

VISTASP M. KARBHARI, PRESIDENT
THE UNIVERSITY OF TEXAS AT ARLINGTON

NO GREATER OPPORTUNITY

IN OCTOBER 1989, the Loma Prieta earthquake struck Northern California at the start of Game 3 of the World Series between the San Francisco Giants and the Oakland A's. It was a terrible tragedy—dozens of people died and billions of dollars' worth of damage was inflicted upon buildings, roads, and infrastructure in the Bay Area. During the twenty seconds of intense shaking, I was at work while my wife, Carmel, and our two young daughters were at home.

Through it all, one primary question occupied my mind—was my family, twelve miles to the east, safe? We didn't have cellphones in those days, so it took some time to reach them on our home phone. I eventually found they were fine, but frightened. Books had fallen off of shelves, picture frames had shattered on the floor, and some of the walls in our house had cracked.

As my personal concerns eased, my professional interest began to mount. Why? Because at the time, I was an assistant professor of structural engineering at the University of California, Berkeley, with a focus on earthquakes, and Loma Prieta was the biggest earthquake to hit the Bay Area since 1906.

In the months and years that followed, the Bay Area

would become a laboratory for me, my graduate students, and quite a few undergraduate students. Throughout their academic studies, my students had gained their engineering knowledge through lectures, projects, and research, but Loma Prieta changed that. Now, the urban landscape was transfigured. Buildings and bridges had been heavily damaged, and some had collapsed. And we were able to go directly to the scenes of the destruction to learn about what happened and figure out why.

I have two vivid memories of that time. The first is of the San Francisco–Oakland Bay Bridge—the longest bridge in the area. A fifty-foot section of the concrete roadway had collapsed, creating a huge gap in the middle of a vital transportation artery that carries hundreds of thousands of vehicles a day. We wanted to understand why that particular section had failed and how safe the rest of the bridge was. My students spent quite a bit of time investigating it with other UC Berkeley faculty members, and they made important discoveries. But in addition to the knowledge gained, I still think back on what it was like to stand on the deserted bridge without traffic, on the precipice of the damaged section, looking down at the bay waters hundreds of feet below. It was a wake-up call to all of us, a reminder of how important it is to build safe structures for the benefit of all people.

My other memory is of driving down to Santa Cruz, close to the earthquake's epicenter, with a car full of students to inspect the damage in that city. We spent an afternoon at the Pacific Garden Mall, observing how the masonry buildings had responded to the shaking of the ground and the sandy soil that had liquefied. We took measurements and collected valuable data. I will always remember, more than anything else, the people who congregated at the mall, simply wanting to know when it would be safe for them to occupy their homes and businesses again.

Throughout our investigations, students were able to gain a greater understanding of the consequences of natural disasters on people and on society. It is nearly always the case that low-income neighborhoods are disproportionately affected by earthquakes, floods, and other extreme events. My students saw this firsthand. They met and spoke with the people who had lost so much: the people for whom, in reality, structural engineers work. It provided motivation for them to gain a deeper understanding of their discipline so that they could go out into the world and make use of their knowledge and skills.

Today, nearly three decades later, many of these students have had impactful careers as engineers, and I'm sure the memories of the Loma Prieta earthquake are still as fresh in their minds as they are in mine. By getting involved and learning from this natural disaster, my students were transformed as engineers. As a professor, I learned that there is no greater opportunity for teaching and learning than one that requires students to engage, participate, and feel—that touches their hearts and minds.

> There is no greater opportunity for teaching and learning than one that requires students to engage, participate, and feel.

GREGORY FENVES, PRESIDENT
THE UNIVERSITY OF TEXAS AT AUSTIN

THE DAY I BECAME A GOOD STUDENT

I WAS ALWAYS an okay student—managed to graduate from Princeton with honors—but I didn't become a good student until my first year of graduate school.

I was working in a research lab at the University of Virginia. Among my labmates were two "terribly old" guys in their late twenties who had military experience. They were highly methodical in their work: they came in before 8:00 a.m.; they worked, worked, worked throughout the day; and they left after 5:00 p.m.

Not so for me.

I'd come and go throughout the day, including weekends, and was just as likely to be working at midnight as at noon.

Early in my first semester in graduate school, I had a project due to a teacher who also happened to be my master's thesis adviser and the director of the lab in which I was working. When it came time to turn in our reports, my two "terribly old" friends turned in beautiful papers. They were typed, albeit with handwritten equations, and the computer output was cut down from the old oversized fan-fold pages to fit into an 8½-by-11 format.

Not so for me.

My report was entirely handwritten, and I had clipped my fan-fold computer output to the report. My handwriting, by the way, is not so good. My professor took one look at my less-than-impressive report and threw it back at me, saying, "I'm not going to read this mess." Only he didn't say "mess."

It was a defining moment for me. I decided that I needed to emulate my older, more professional labmates, starting with a redo of that report.

More importantly, I immediately adopted their work habits. I came in before 8:00 a.m.; worked, worked, worked throughout the day; and left after 5:00 p.m. It turns out you can get a lot done that way, and I still had weekends and evening hours when the crunch was on.

An interesting epilogue came at the University of California, Berkeley, where I did my doctoral work. I had a desk in a bullpen where almost every other graduate student was an advisee of the then department head.

Although I wasn't yet "terribly old," I was now the one with the disciplined work habits. I soon came to know that the department head would drift through the room at around 8:15 a.m. Inevitably, I was the only one there, and we would nod at each other.

After a couple of weeks of this, the department head came over and said something to the effect of: "Who are you? I come here every morning hoping to see my students, but I never find them. I only find you. Who are you?"

So I told him who I was, and it launched a brief daily conversation, lasting maybe fifteen seconds. It was not hard to admire the department head, a tremendous scholar, as well as a pleasant and energetic man who would later go on to become the UC Berkeley chancellor.

When I completed my PhD, the department head did me a great honor. I got to present on the department's colloquium series, which was usually reserved for well-established scholars visiting UC Berkeley. I had many enjoyable encounters with the department head/chancellor in the years that followed, and always felt honored to be regarded as a friend.

I have often thought back to that singular moment at the University of Virginia when I became a good student, computer fan-fold paper flapping through the air. One might say that I was being graded that day by my adviser. The teaching, however, came from the two "terribly old" students sitting next to me. From them, I learned what disciplined students do.

> The teaching came from the two "terribly old" students sitting next to me. From them, I learned what disciplined students do.

You know, good students.

RICHARD C. BENSON, PRESIDENT
THE UNIVERSITY OF TEXAS AT DALLAS

THE ROAD TO SOCIAL MOBILITY

OVER THE PAST THIRTY YEARS, the University of Texas at El Paso has focused intensely on our public university responsibility to offer both access and excellence to the historically underserved, predominantly Hispanic, modest-income population of the surrounding region. To that end, we have set access goals to grow UT El Paso's enrollment, sought to ensure its alignment with the demographics of the regional population we serve (80 percent Hispanic), and increased the degree completion rates of those who enroll. We also set aggressive excellence goals to ensure that the education we offer students enables them, upon graduation, to compete successfully with their more affluent peers in more prestigious settings.

> Our students' competitiveness required enhancing their confidence and self-esteem by valuing their many assets.

We also recognized that our students' competitiveness would require enhancing their confidence and self-esteem by valuing and building on their many assets as well as being more intentional about broadening and integrating their range of experiences at UT El Paso. We made this the focus of our Quality Enhancement Plan (QEP) for the Southern Association of Colleges and Schools Commission on Colleges (SACSCOC) five years ago and are now implementing it as the UTEP Edge. In the process, we have drawn on the diverse perspectives of our own faculty and staff, as many of them, like our students, grew up in families of modest means and were the first to attend college. As a first-generation student myself, I have enjoyed this opportunity to reflect on the factors that played a significant role in defining my own challenges and successes.

I was seventeen years old when I graduated from a blue-collar public high school in St. Louis, where the focus was on preparing graduates for the workforce. The boys were expected to become apprentices in the trade unions—electricians, plumbers, or carpenters—and the girls were expected to marry those boys, perhaps after a brief stint in a clerical job. Enrolling in college was not a topic of conversation, and most courses were neither rigorous nor taught with passion. I did not take the SAT or explore with teachers or counselors specific post-secondary opportunities. Like my fellow graduates, I believed that my next step was to enter the workforce, and I did. I was soon hired as a switchboard operator and receptionist at a large industrial company—I was the Lily Tomlin of Nordberg Manufacturing! After a month of connecting, transferring, and disconnecting calls, I was bored by the repetitive set of tasks I was hired to perform and frightened by the thought that my future could be swallowed up in a switchboard box.

It was then that I made a bold decision to explore the possibility of going to college, and I learned that I basically had two options: St. Louis University (SLU) or Washington University (WU), both private. There were no public universities in St. Louis at that time, and I couldn't afford to go away to school. I chose SLU because it was more accessible by public transportation, and its $375 per semester tuition was $50 lower than Washington University's. Less than confidently, I went to the SLU Admissions Office to inquire about enrolling. In spite of the poor reputation of my high school, I was admitted, but I was told that I'd have to work very hard to compete with the other SLU students. Many of them were graduates of private high schools with college preparatory curricula and standards.

I enrolled and began a four-year marathon to catch up with my peers. I'd attend classes in the morning, work as a typist in the afternoon, and study relentlessly in the evening and on weekends. I had no free time for extracurricular activities, partly because I did have a lot of catching up to do, and partly because, despite some early evidence that I was at least holding my own, the possibility of failure was constantly looming. Deep down, I didn't have confidence in my capacity to compete successfully in the university environment, and quitting my job—even one I disliked—to enroll at SLU represented a very high-stakes bet.

Except for the chronic stage fright I suffered in an Oral Interpretation course, I greatly enjoyed and was inspired by nearly all my classes taught by SLU's accomplished teacher-scholars. I was especially impacted by two of them, both Jesuits, who taught Spanish language and literature and whose highly animated classroom presentations and active engagement with students created the most exhilarating learning environment I had ever experienced. They made Spanish language and literature come alive for me. I eagerly prepared for, looked forward to, and energetically participated in all their classes. Those two outstanding teachers not only taught me Spanish, but also enabled me to develop my self-confidence and discover my deep passion for learning—and later teaching—languages and linguistics.

I completed my bachelor's degree in Spanish with honors, an unimaginable outcome when I had enrolled four years earlier. Even more unimaginable was being awarded upon graduation a Fulbright fellowship to study Portuguese in Brazil, an experience that forever changed the trajectory of my life.

As I think back about what mattered most in my educational experience, three factors stand out. First, the low expectations of my blue-collar high school came dangerously close to ending my educational journey. Second, despite my weak pre-college educational preparation, financial constraints, and lack of self-confidence, St. Louis University gave me the chance to prove myself, both to them and—perhaps most importantly—to me. And last, but certainly not least, two talented and dedicated SLU faculty members engaged me fully in discovering and developing my own joy and passion for learning. They paved the way for my deeply fulfilling academic career and the special privilege of working every day for the past thirty years to ensure that UT El Paso plays as significant a role in our students' lives as SLU did in mine.

DIANA NATALICIO, PRESIDENT
THE UNIVERSITY OF TEXAS AT EL PASO

THE LIFE-CHANGING POWER
OF A SINGLE CONVERSATION

I GOT MARRIED when I was only eighteen and soon found myself with two babies, too many bills, and not enough paycheck. I instinctively knew that the only way to significantly improve my situation was to find some way to graduate from college. It would take me ten years to become the first person in my family to earn a university degree.

My journey was fraught with many obstacles. One of the most pressing obstacles involved money—or, more accurately, lack of money. I will be a senior citizen when my college loans are paid off—true story!

Time was another obstacle—I spent most of my college days working a full-time job, caring for two sweet babies, and juggling classes on very little sleep. After work I would tuck my little ones in bed and drive either to class or to the local Shoney's restaurant to study, because they stayed open until 2:00 a.m. I studied there so much that they saved my booth in the back and sent free strawberry pie every night to help me through the midnight stretch.

The obstacle that affected me most was the paralyzing fear of failure—the fear that I was not smart enough. In reality, I knew that I had not prepared academically for college in high school because I had never planned to go. This was back in the "olden" days before common core requirements. I wasn't required to take much math in high school, so I didn't.

This brings me to the story about a very special teacher who is the reason I am where I am. I started my ten-year journey at a community college. I worked really hard and was making slow but solid progress. I saved algebra for the latest possible time because I had such a fear of math—and with good reason. I didn't even know that a negative times a negative is a positive! I was lost in class and struggling to keep up. I remember very vividly the day I got my first algebra test back—I can still see the bright red mark, 62 F, on the page. It was the first time I'd failed a test in college and I was devastated. I felt an embarrassing sense of shame and panic—hot tears were streaming down my face. I went to Professor Davis's office clutching the evidence of failure in my hands. Professor Davis was a great teacher, but she was not exactly known for her warmth. She was a small, stern-looking woman, a real no-nonsense kind of professor who was probably overworked and underpaid.

There I was sitting in her office, a grown mother of two sobbing uncontrollably, mumbling incoherently about how I was going to quit, that I wasn't smart enough and didn't know why I ever thought I could do it. I was emotionally and financially spent. This was my breaking point. She patiently listened to me sob for a long time.

Finally, she stopped me and asked for the test back. So I slid the test across the desk to her. She very dramatically rolled her eyes, took out her bright red sharpie, and crossed out the F and replaced it with a D. She rolled her eyes again and slid the test back to me. She looked me in the eye sternly and said—"there—stop your crying—you didn't fail the test."

It is hard to articulate the significance of this one moment that had the power to change the trajectory of my life. It was such a small act of kindness, and I bet she never gave it another thought, but thirty years later I still weep every time I tell the story. I don't know why not having an F on my test was so important to my fragile state of mind, but it was, and she recognized it.

I was going to drop out of college that day, but her wisdom, kindness, and support gave me the confidence to stop crying and get back to work. She told me I was smart enough, and as it turns out, she was right. Almost ten years after that day, I would go on to graduate with high honors from Auburn University with a degree in economics and finance, and I would use my hard-earned math skills to become the chief financial officer in several major university systems before becoming president. Thank you, Professor Davis, wherever you are!

> I was going to drop out of college, but her wisdom, kindness, and support gave me the confidence to get back to work.

SANDRA K. WOODLEY, PRESIDENT
THE UNIVERSITY OF TEXAS PERMIAN BASIN

THE TEACHER WHO WOULDN'T
ANSWER MY QUESTIONS

THE TEACHER I LEARNED the most from in college wouldn't answer my questions. In my first semester as a graduate student, I took a seminar in lexicography. I was especially excited about the professor in the course, a well-known linguist who had a reputation for being a superb teacher. As I listened intently during the first class, I had a number of questions about various topics that were raised and approached the professor after class to ask him those questions. To my surprise and consternation, he wouldn't answer them. Instead, he simply told me how to discover the answers for myself.

I was more than a little frustrated: I just wanted answers to my questions, not more work to do. After all, I was a busy graduate student. Before the next class period, I did the research needed to answer the questions, but I decided on a new strategy for any additional questions I had: I'd ask them during class. He'd have to answer my questions then. I was fooling myself, though. When I (and other students) asked questions, he answered the same way he had answered me earlier, "Here's how you would find the answer to that question." He would then proceed to explain how to do the research needed to answer the question. Although I remained frustrated, I was interested enough in the material to do the research necessary to answer my questions.

After a few class periods, I actually found myself looking forward to these little mini research projects—and not worried at all about the professor's unwillingness to answer questions. I also found myself learning much more than I ever dreamed I could learn. By the end of the semester, I realized that I not only had learned a lot about lexicography, but had also learned something even more important: I had learned how to learn.

It's no accident that my first scholarly publication came out of that seminar in lexicography. In the course I learned how to create knowledge, and I fell in love with knowledge creation—and with research, the mechanism by which we create knowledge. It is also no accident that in this seminar I discovered the principle that was to become the cornerstone of my teaching philosophy: the best way to learn is by doing. When I became a faculty member a few years later, I worked hard to develop courses organized around the principle of learning by doing. Courses that help students discover how to answer their own questions, that teach students not just content but how to learn, are the courses that are the most helpful later in life. The substance of courses and of disciplines changes over time, but knowing how to learn, along with a fascination with the process of discovery, lasts forever. I owe this insight (and much of my career) to the professor who refused to answer my questions.

> The teacher I learned the most from in college wouldn't answer my questions.

GUY BAILEY, PRESIDENT
THE UNIVERSITY OF TEXAS RIO GRANDE VALLEY

"DREAM NO SMALL DREAMS": INSPIRING STUDENTS TO REACH FOR THE STARS

Dream no small dreams for they have no power to move the hearts of men.

—JOHANN WOLFGANG VON GOETHE

IN ALL MY YEARS as a teacher, researcher, and administrator, I've had one fundamental goal: encouraging students to dream big.

For so many students, life's many distractions and responsibilities get in the way of visualizing where they want to go. They are so dedicated to managing their classwork, employment responsibilities, and time with their families that there is hardly a moment to think beyond the next day, let alone the next year or the decades to come.

As a first-year student at Tufts University back in 1975, I had no idea how to set big goals. Even worse, I was floundering in school—I was a lousy student. After a less-than-stellar first year, I decided to drop out and reevaluate.

One year later I returned and met the faculty mentor who would change the course of my life.

I had always loved science, so I decided to take a class with Dr. Jan Pechenik, a highly regarded marine biologist specializing in the study of invertebrates. Dr. Pechenik had made a name for himself with his research about a rare gastropod called the slipper limpet, a kind of sea snail.

He must have seen something in me I didn't see in myself. Dr. Pechenik brought me into his lab and invited me to join in his research. I chose to study the larval form of adult slipper limpets, something very few scientists were studying at the time. The thought that I was creating new knowledge was thrilling.

My time in Dr. Pechenik's lab sparked my *AHA!* moment—the realization that I cared about the scientific process, and that I had the passion and capacity to become a scientist. I reinvented myself as a student. I found myself driven to learn, not for grades or accolades, but because I was truly fascinated by the work I was doing.

I was so hungry for more; I sought out other opportunities to develop my passion and did a senior research project at Northeastern University's Marine Science Center. On Saturday mornings, I found myself getting up early to visit the Harvard Museum of Comparative Zoology, spending what scarce resources I had making photocopies of articles from marine biology journals in their collection.

I completed my senior project and, after graduation, continued to develop my skills as a researcher at the Woods Hole Oceanographic Institution. All this work eventually launched my career as a research faculty member and center director at the University of New Hampshire. The rest, as they say, is history.

None of this would have transpired without Dr. Pechenik taking the time to show me the possibilities of a scientific life. His encouragement, and his belief in the power of experiential learning, helped me find my big dreams.

As faculty members, our role is so much bigger than

just imparting course content. It's our responsibility and privilege to help students find those magical moments, the genesis of dreams. Personal interactions and experiential learning opportunities are obvious pathways, but it can be as simple as encouraging students to get involved on campus and to take time to explore cocurricular and extracurricular offerings.

> It's our responsibility and privilege to help students find those magical moments, the genesis of dreams.

Dr. Pechenik knew how to provide the right environment to spark my *AHA!* moment. My aim is to do the same with as many students as I meet. Whether you are just starting out in your teaching career or someone like me who has moved on to the administrative ranks, all of us have the capacity to create the right settings for *AHA!* moments big and small. No matter how busy they may be, all students deserve the opportunity to find their intellectual spark.

All of us who choose the academic life care deeply about learning, discovery, and mentoring. We all have such a profound ability to transform lives. As mentors, especially, we can help students realize that *this* is their moment—their time to dream big dreams—and help them find their pathways.

Good luck in all your endeavors!

TAYLOR EIGHMY, PRESIDENT
THE UNIVERSITY OF TEXAS AT SAN ANTONIO

MAKING A DIFFERENCE

MY LIFE HAS BEEN FILLED with teachers who have had a profound and constructive influence on my journey to the present day. Two of my most transformational experiences occurred somewhat early in my educational development and helped me understand the importance of communication.

One fortifying influence was Mrs. Beverly Hamlin. My fourth-grade teacher in the gifted and talented education program, Mrs. Hamlin was an ardent devotee of the art of communication, and she relished developing her students' oratorical skills. She guided me through competitions to sharpen my skills.

Mrs. Hamlin's class laid the fertile groundwork in which my love for the spoken word flourished, and it is my belief that my effectiveness as an educator and a leader is due, in great part, to her guidance. In leadership, we must be able to effectively communicate our vision and our ideas to a team in a way that will motivate and inspire. As educators, we must communicate information in a way that engages students and helps them comprehend it.

Another significant experience transpired in a college course called Argumentation and Debate. It was taught by

Professor Mike Bauer, and it enhanced my comprehension of communication. I had engaged in public speaking for years and found it to be fulfilling, but his class was about public thinking—the ability to engage people in a public forum and to listen to their ideas and theories. Then you must process that information to formulate your own opinions and respond in an appropriate and effective manner.

Professor Bauer steered my debate team to a number-one national ranking in parliamentary debate. Under his guidance, I was recognized as one of the nation's top ten speakers. These honors might not have been possible had it not been for the indelible impressions that both Professor Bauer and Mrs. Hamlin had made on me.

They endowed me with communication skills that would propel me toward success in my life and career. They demonstrated how teachers can chart the course for students and help define their educational and professional achievements. Under their tutelage I developed a deep, intuitive understanding of the importance of communication in student success.

> Teachers can chart the course for students and help define their educational and professional achievements.

As an educator, I understand that it is imperative for students to develop a strong command of the spoken word. They must be able to communicate clear, substantive, and compelling thoughts. As we train our students to be great in their chosen fields, it is crucial that we prepare them to be competent communicators. This will enhance their probability for success. That is the hallmark of a great educator.

MICHAEL V. TIDWELL, PRESIDENT
THE UNIVERSITY OF TEXAS AT TYLER

ACADEMY CONTRIBUTORS' BIOGRAPHIES

BETH BRUNK-CHAVEZ is dean of the Extended University and professor of Rhetoric and Writing Studies at the University of Texas at El Paso. She was president of the UT System Academy of Distinguished Teachers from 2017 to 2019 and is a 2009 recipient of the Regents' Outstanding Teaching Award. Her administrative work focuses on building and sustaining fully online degree programs and online course development. Her research areas include writing program administration, writing assessment, digital composition, teaching with technologies, and multi-language writers. She currently serves on the executive board of the Council of Writing Program Administration.

KEVIN COKLEY holds the Oscar and Anne Mauzy Regents Professorship for Educational Research and Development in the College of Education at the University of Texas at Austin. He is a Fellow of the UT System Academy of Distinguished Teachers and director of the Institute for Urban Policy Research and Analysis. His research and teaching is broadly in the area of African American psychology. He studies the psychosocial experiences of students of color and is currently exploring the impostor phenomenon and its relationship to mental health and academic outcomes. He is the recipient of the 2014 Regents' Outstanding Teaching Award.

DIANA DOMINGUEZ is a professor of English at the University of Texas Rio Grande Valley where she teaches primarily ancient to medieval, women's, and children's and adolescent literature. Her research is primarily focused on early twentieth-century American series for teen girls and depictions of diversity in contemporary picture books. She is a 2014 recipient of the Regents' Outstanding Teaching Award and, in 2015, was named a Fellow of the UT System Academy of Distinguished Teachers. She has published and presented scholarly and creative work regionally, nationally, and internationally.

KAREN HUXTABLE began teaching in 1988 and has served as associate director of the UT Dallas Center for Teaching and Learning since its launch in 2016. She is a Senior Lecturer III for Behavioral and Brain Sciences (BBS) and has taught educational, social, and developmental psychology to nearly 11,000 students since 2000. She served as BBS Teaching Support Coordinator from 2012 to 2015. She received the Excellence in Teaching Award in 2005, the Seniors' Choice Award in 2009, and the Regents' Outstanding Teaching Award in 2013, and she is a 2017 inductee to the UT System Academy of Distinguished Teachers.

MARY MCNAUGHTON-CASSILL is a professor of clinical psychology at the University of Texas at San Antonio. Her research focuses on understanding the psychosocial sources of stress among college students and the relationship between news media exposure and stress. She is the author of *Mind the Gap: Managing Stress in the Modern World* and the editor of *Adapt and Overcome: Essays on the Veteran Student*. As the director of the Educational Mental Health Initiatives at UTSA, she has been working with faculty, staff, and students to improve mental health awareness and responses on campus.

ALEX R. PIQUERO is Ashbel Smith Professor of Criminology and associate dean for Graduate Programs in the School of Economic, Political and Policy Sciences at the University of Texas at Dallas. His research interests include criminal careers, criminological theory, and quantitative research methods. He currently serves as editor of *Justice Evaluation Journal*. He has received several research, teaching, and service awards and is Fellow of both the American Society of Criminology and the Academy of Criminal Justice Sciences. In 2014, he received the Regents' Outstanding Teaching Award, and in 2018 he was named to the UT System Academy of Distinguished Teachers.

KENNETH ROEMER is a Piper Professor, Distinguished Teaching Professor, and Distinguished Scholar Professor at the University of Texas at Arlington, a National Endowment for the Humanities grantee, and a Pulitzer Prize nominee. He has guest-lectured at Harvard University and in twelve different countries. His eight books focus on Native American and utopian literature.

BARBARA SHIPMAN is passionate about teaching mathematics in ways that inspire students to enjoy it, be creative with it, and understand it deeply. She is an associate professor and Distinguished Teaching Professor at the University of Texas at Arlington, where she has received many teaching awards. To complement her work in differential geometry, she enjoys rethinking foundational concepts in new and insightful ways and presenting engaging workshops and colloquia for mathematical and general audiences. She plays the violin and viola, spends active time outdoors, and enjoys learning about plants, animals, and geology.

LIST OF STUDENTS BY INSTITUTION

THE UNIVERSITY OF TEXAS AT ARLINGTON
Lea Arista
Michael Camele
Alexander Trent Christensen
John Martin Crowley
Erica Davis
Misty Martin
Allison Piercy
Courtney Weston

THE UNIVERSITY OF TEXAS AT AUSTIN
Mariagrazia Arata
Aarti Bhat
Gabe Colombo
Rachel Diebner
Bianca Hsieh
Surabi Rao
Julieta Scalo
Nicole Sun
George Walters

THE UNIVERSITY OF TEXAS AT DALLAS
Delia Appiah Mensah
Leena Berriche

Jessica Goodwin
Marissa Tavallaee

THE UNIVERSITY OF TEXAS AT EL PASO
Brianna Barreiro
Alma Carolina Escobosa
Pema Euden
Edward Gunderson
Holly McDonald
Hope Nelson
Michelle Perez
Ricardo Ramirez Jr.
Carl Ryan Robins

THE UNIVERSITY OF TEXAS PERMIAN BASIN
Victoria Inman-Hinesly

THE UNIVERSITY OF TEXAS RIO GRANDE VALLEY
Robert Bujanos
Jessica Haught

THE UNIVERSITY OF TEXAS AT SAN ANTONIO
Melina Acosta
Tyler Klein
Cory Knight
Saifa Pirani

THE UNIVERSITY OF TEXAS AT TYLER
Carol DeGrasse
Radley Feiner
Christy Hjorth
Jeffrey Michael King
Lena Liedtke
Mary Rose Pihlak
Trev Franklin Thompson